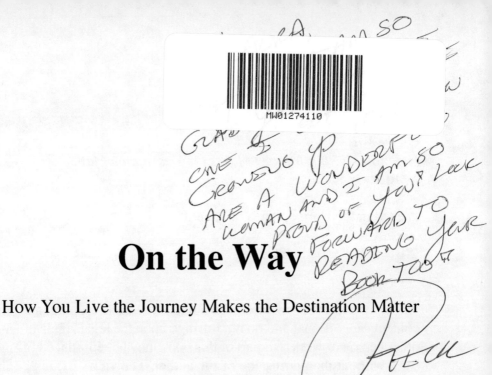

On the Way

How You Live the Journey Makes the Destination Matter

By

Rick Grieve

<u>Includes Questions for Study and Reflection</u>

PRESS

ACKNOWLEDGMENTS

This book began over 4 years ago with a simple devotion in our church staff chapel. Since that time I have lived the journey from inspiration to publication. And let me tell you, it required more than I bargained for. I have probably learned more in my travels than I even know. But I know this. I still have much to learn. Taking a piece of my own advice from Stop #7, I would like to thank so many who have invested and believed in me through this process.

- God allowed me to serve with two amazing Senior Pastors as I wrote this book. Thank you Pastor Ross and Pastor Paul for your encouragement and mentoring, you have both helped me grow in so many ways, on the way.
- Special thanks to the pastors and staff at First Assembly of God who listened patiently to many of the thoughts in this book and prodded me not to give up on the dream (Pastor Jim included even though you've moved West).
- Tammy for your support, editing talents, and timely advice.
- Joanna for mentoring me through this process and taking time out of your busy life to speak into mine.
- To the Church Body at First Assembly of God who has never stopped believing in me and this project. Thank you for allowing me to teach these lessons and learn from wise and seasoned travelers.
- Tamara and Will; I love you both more than life itself. You have put up with Dad's face in the computer and loved him

through the many edits and brain cramps. You are what make my journey so wonderful!

- Jesus Christ – you are the same yesterday, today, and forever. You are my compass on this journey and a constant friend through every road. Thank you for loving me and never giving up on me.

TABLE OF CONTENTS:

PART ONE ... PACKING FOR THE PROCESS

PART TWO ... MOVING OUT

DESTINATION DRIVEN OR JOURNEY FOCUSED?

I was in love. After years of searching, desperately trying to find that special person that would complete me, the journey was over. Rejection and disillusionment had almost caused me to give up hope, but there she was. Gracefully striding down the aisle of the church, her smile lighting up the room, her piercing blue eyes sending tremors through my body to the heart she had already captured. I'll never forget standing at the front of the church as the congregation joined me in speechless awe; captivated by the beautiful sight of the woman I would spend the rest of my life with. She was stunning, breath-taking perfection, without the slightest detectable personality fault. But it didn't last long.

Soon after the vows we're spoken and the promises were given, I made a painful discovery. My bride was flawed. A hidden character deficiency tucked deep beneath the surface of apparent flawlessness. But such secrets can only be concealed for so long.

You see, unlike me, gifted with the knowledge that road trips are best taken quickly and without stopping, the love of my life did not have this same understanding. Raised in Montana hours away from the nearest mall, Tamara viewed traveling as an opportunity to create memories (God forbid).

My new wife found it necessary to stop for such frivolous activities as eating, drinking, sightseeing, and yes, even bathroom breaks. I must admit, I used to think that there was something wrong with Tamara — that somehow it was my duty to enlighten her to the proper way to travel. "You see, honey" I tried to explain, "every time we stop all the cars we've passed, catch up. I am obligated by the 'Destination Code Book' to respond. We must not let them win. Stopping causes defeat and forces me to speed. Besides we've already wasted 4 minutes and 42 seconds picking up a snack and 6 minutes and," I paused to look at my watch, "32, 33, 34, 35 seconds for this potty break."

> *"Life doesn't come to us like a math problem. It comes to us the way that a story does, scene by scene. What will happen next? You don't get to know – you have to enter in, take the journey as it comes. Life unfolds like a drama." John Eldredge from his book* Epic

Well, fifteen years later, and the one being taught now is this stubborn destination enamored husband. I've begun to take driving a little less seriously (though my flare for the dramatic hasn't seemed to waver much). Not to say I'm reckless, I just don't make getting to the destination as swiftly as possible my only goal. I now try to relax and see the sights.

At times my journey focus is a bit sketchy and I have my relapses. The weekend I chauffeured my wife and ten teenage girls to the mall was a severe test. Going from store to store, I learned more about the countless shades of pink then I care to admit (there's three dozen, I think). Flight delays and unscheduled counseling sessions still provoke the destination side of me at times, but I am trying and my wife still holds to hope. Perhaps by the end of this book I may have reached wholeness.

DESTINATION DRIVEN OR JOURNEY FOCUSED?

Many live out life with the same focus I once had in my traveling. As I talk to people, more and more it seems a common thread runs through the middle of all the frustration and activity. Specifically, the need to be reminded that life is a journey, not only a destination.

A 2006 Associated Press poll exposed this truth. "(We are) an impatient Nation, that gets antsy after five minutes on hold on the phone and 15 minutes max in a line ...In short, Americans want it NOW." The report indicated whether in the city or the country, young or old, the typical American feels "time-poor."[1]

One woman responded to this dilemma with the following thoughts, "The ultimate paradox is by trying to do everything right we miss the most important part of life. And sensing we are missing something drives us to do more."[2] In agreement another explained, "Women are spread too thin."[3] And these Ladies aren't alone. One man expressed, "It's like a disease or an addiction, I just can't seem to slow down."

For some of us the symptoms show up pretty early in life. Not long after the moment we escape the nine-month prison of our mother's womb, something surfaces in the character and personality of each individual. Observe with me the peaceful child who sleeps the entire night only days after leaving the hospital. She reveals calm tranquil qualities, patiently soaking in every image and experience.

Now open your eyes to her not so docile counterpart. In the corner crib ... do you see him? There he is, the precious baby who wakes up every hour, unable and unwilling to sit still, even in his dreams. Though not an inescapable sign of their futures, these two infants expose a very real condition found in the adult world they will soon enter.

There are those that live life and those that survive it ... the "Destination Driven" and the "Journey Focused." Whether we designate people's personalities as Type A, Type B, or Type ABC, the labels matter little. What matters is that those living destination driven miss much. They miss life.

Destination Driven describes the person who is preoccupied with arriving and achieving. Enjoying the process is difficult because they're consumed with the final result. Goals and accomplishments tend to rule over people and relationships. The Destination Driven are often in a hurry. *Key words: Goal, Go, Get there.*

To the contrary the *Journey Focused* are observant; focusing on what is happening around them, looking for the lesson and beauty in every moment. For the final result to mean anything the process must be enjoyed. People and relationships override goals and tasks. The Journey Focused learn from life's interruptions. *Key Words: Look, Learn, Live there.*

> *"Pursue your passion, but don't forget to have fun!"*
> — *Dr. David Jeremiah from his book Life Wide Open*

JESUS ... ON THE WAY

Many of the greatest moments in the greatest story ever told occurred "on the way." The life of our Master was abundant – filled with amazing miracles, awe inspiring teaching and incredible rendezvous. Yet the majority of them occurred not at his destination, but in the journey.

In Mark chapter 5, Jesus is traveling to the home of a religious ruler named Jairus. Jairus' daughter is very ill, so Jesus sets his coarse directly toward her bed side. With a planned destination in mind Jesus made his way through the packed streets. On the way - a feeble sickly woman reached out and touched the hem of Jesus' robe. Instantly, she received the healing that all her wealth and twelve years of doctor visits could not provide. Her faith made her well and her touch received Jesus recognition and praise. But she was not the destination. She was merely a spot along Jesus' journey, a moment – on the way.

Next up, Jesus and his disciples took a little trip to the villages surrounding Caesarea Philippi. It is in this journey that Jesus asked his disciples the greatest question anyone will ever answer, "Who do you say that I am?" No other question is more critical than this, the fate of every soul hinges on the answer. The disciples are picking rocks from their sandals and guessing how far till they reach town and Jesus pops the question (see Mark 8). Yet His inquiry comes not in church nor seated at a meal nor around a meeting table - he asked it, on the way.

"The way of Jesus is a journey, not a destination" — Rob Bell from his book Velvet Elvis

Then there was that famous meeting at the well in Samaria. Jesus struck up a conversation with a woman of less than reputable character and past. A "chance" meeting at a communal watering hole that changed her eternal destination and produced "many who put their trust in him," yet Jesus was only "passing through" (see John 4). This woman's life was turned around and an entire town turned up-side-down, all because of a little rest stop in Jesus' pursuit toward another destination.

And who could forget Jesus' betrayal announcement "on the way" to Jerusalem (Mark 10:32), or the disciples' argument over who was the greatest and Jesus challenging response — these occurred on the journey, too (Mark 9:34). They saw Jesus walk on water and calm the storm with a word. But they were only there because they were "headed to the other side."

Even in his death so much happened from the arrest to his final cry. Words spoken, lives impacted, history altered long before he breathed his final breath – all on the way to the cross. Now, you may view some of those events as minor, but I assure you that Simon Peter, Simon the Cyrene and the thief who died paradise-bound saw those "on the ways" as quite significant.

If this is true of the life of Jesus then maybe it's true of ours as well. If so, then pursuing life without learning from the process has the potential of costing us a great deal.

THE HIGH COST OF DRIVENNESS

The busier we become the less we notice. Time with God, time with others, time to take in the important things on the way, are sacrificed on the altar of achievement. The journey digresses into time crunches, task to complete, and schedules to keep. Charles E. Hummel writes in his profound booklet, *Tyranny of the Urgent*, "We live in constant tension between the urgent and the important ... The appeal of these demands seems irresistible, and they devour our energy. But in the light of eternity their prominence fades. With a sense of loss we recall the important tasks that have been shunted aside."

Licensed psychologist, Don R. Powell warns, "With the threat of terrorism, uncertain economic times, broken marriages and wayward children to worry about, I'd say that we have a whole series of events coming together now that are more profound than any other time in history." As president of the American Institute for Preventive Medicine, Dr. Powell provides stress management training to corporate employees.[4] He understands the burden of business – the disease of the destination driven.

Serious health risks as well as migraine headaches, muscle tension, high blood pressure, insomnia, ulcers, and rheumatoid arthritis inflict many anxious and over worked Americans.[5]

- Forty-three percent of all adults suffer adverse health effects from stress
- Seventy-five percent to 90 percent of all physician office visits are for stress-related ailments and complaints.
- Stress is linked to the six leading causes of death — heart disease, cancer, lung ailments, accidents, cirrhosis of the liver, and suicide.
- There's even evidence linking stress with premature aging. Researchers at the University of California, San Francisco found that prolonged psychological stress affects molecules that are believed to play a role in cellular aging and, possibly, the onset of disease. [6]

Feeling a little stressed? Good, now let me guide you to the solution. Only you hold the keys to change yourself! If we don't start living the present differently we're libel to lose the future. It's time for us to rise up and seize the journey, not just strive after the destination.

THE REWARDS AND THE RISKS

God created us to enjoy the process of life - not rush to its end. The dates engraved on our tombstone say little, it is the hyphen in between that tells the whole story. There is much between our birth and our burial, maybe God puts that big span of time there for a reason … so enjoy it.

Think about it for a minute, what are we rushing for any way? All that waits at the end of this life before eternity is a pine box and a six foot drop. Why do we seem so eager to finish the job?

I often hear people say, "I just can't wait …!" We seem to be looking forward to something or sometime or someplace we are not currently in. Sixth graders want to be in junior high, high schoolers want to be in college, singles want to be married, the married want to have kids, those who live in the city want to live in the country, those who have an apartment want a house of their own, employees want promotions, employers want retirement, and so on it goes.

In the 1980's the music group Lover Boy sang a song that was entitled, *Everybody's Working For the Weekend.* What a waste, throwing 70 percent of life down the trash, savoring only a morsel of God's intended feast. Saturday and Sunday may be more enjoyable, but I guarantee, God has much to show us in the other five.

We live most of life in the future. We miss "the present" of the present, and all the amazing gifts hidden inside. Yet the Apostle Paul told us the secret to living was learning, "to be content whatever the circumstances." (Philippians 4:11)

In the midst of all this "I can't wait," there are lessons God wants to teach us that we can only learn here, now, in our current circumstances. If we avoid and ignore today in order to daydream about tomorrow, tomorrow we'll wish that yesterday had not gone by so fast.

Over the last few years, little things have begun to capture my attention like never before. Interesting lessons from unusual places jump out and grab hold of me on the way.

> *"Don't be afraid of death, be afraid of the unlived life."*
> *— Natalie Babbitt, from <u>Tuck Everlasting</u>*

At one of our recent travel stops (a new experience for me I assure you) I read a quote at a Union 76 Gas station. It was simple and yet profound (for a gas station sign at least), "Life happens between empty and full." Life is not just a starting point and a destination, life is the "in between."

Have you noticed, or have you just been too busy trying to arrive? God speaks through so many different avenues and uses a variety of instruments to catch our attention. If he could use a donkey in the Old Testament why not a street sign or the voice of your child today? If a really big fish could get a wandering prophet back on track why not a song or statement timely delivered in your daily routine? It will do us a great deal of good if we will listen carefully and watch thoughtfully as we travel.

You'll be amazed how things that used to annoy and frustrate you become divine moments where you touch heaven – and heaven touches you. Bad traffic becomes a needed pause, a gifted moment to be with God. Human error and mistakes become a gateway for God's grace to another traveler in need of understanding and encouragement. Heaven-sent appointments are scheduled everyday if our schedules don't blind us to the possibilities.

"Enjoy the journey and you'll live longer. Enjoy the journey and the life you live will be better. Enjoy the journey and others will enjoy being with you."

Its "on the way" we find our way and get out of God's way! The journey is a masterful teacher in the hands of the Divine craftsman. In the process of life God lights our paths to reveal his will and lead us to his chosen destiny. By living preoccupied and driven for the destination we jeopardize knowing God's guiding hand – a reward we dare not risk. The price could be eternal.

TREASURE SEEKERS, SEIZE THE JOURNEY

Every roadway holds a treasure, every turn, a jewel of immeasurable worth. Those who run the race blind never discover these valuables; those who hurry to the end neither seek nor find them. God beams with pleasure when we treasure the life he gives.   O   n your journey, while passing by, look around and notice the treasures that surround you. Open the voluminous chest of life's experiences.

Study the shimmer of the diamonds of delays and detours forged through the pressure of the unexpected. Hold tight the priceless pure gold of miraculous moments purified through the mundane.

Cradle in your hands the countless gems of humility, the sparkle of temptations avoided, the glow of a life shaped to know God. Cherish the setbacks and successes; difficult situations that will shine brightly in your heavenly crown ... as monuments of God's faithfulness and your obedience.

In her book, *With This Ring: Promises to Keep,* Joanna Weaver retells a story of a Destination Driven man who missed the treasures that lay before him every day.

The legend says that long ago in ancient Persia there lived a man named Ali Hafed. He owned a large farm filled with lush orchards, acres of grain fields, and beautiful gardens. His wife was lovely, and his children brought him great pleasure. Ali Hafed was quite content.

One day a priest came to visit. "Diamonds are to be desired above all else," the wizened old man told Ali, his eyes vibrant, his hands expressive. "If you have diamonds, you'll never want for anything."

The priest's words took root, and Ali became consumed with the translucent jewels – their fire, their depth, their worth. Soon Ali Hafed sold his farm and left his family to search the world for the finest diamonds. He would have them, no matter the cost.

Ali's quest took him all through Europe and down into Africa, but he found nothing that satisfied him. Before long, his money was gone, and his dreams of diamonds lay as shredded as the rags that clothed his body.

Hopeless and discouraged, Ali Hafed stood at the edge of a stormy Barbary Coast bay. Whipped by wind and rain, he stared at a giant tidal wave approaching the shore. But instead of running for safety, Ali calmly walked into the rolling surf and embraced the wave, ending his life.

The man who had purchased Ali Hafed's farm was watering his camel at the garden brook one day. The sun hung brilliant in the cloudless sky as the camel thrust his snout deep into the shallow water. Suddenly a bright glint in the white sand caught the farmer's eye. He bent down and gently brushed the sand away, revealing glistening stones. Diamonds. Scores and scores of diamonds.[7]

There in the brook lay the beginnings of the most magnificent diamond mine in the history of humankind: the Golconda. From its depths would come the largest crown jewels in the world.

Ali Hafed had gone searching the world for diamonds, while all along, the largest and the very best lay under his feet.

As Ali strove to gain what was not his, he lost what he possessed all along. There are many destinations in life, some we never achieve. But the greatest treasures are already ours. They are found in the midst of our journeys, if we will only "clear away the sands of time and busyness," to see them.

God made life to be enjoyed. Jesus said, "I have come that they may have life and have it to the full" (John 10:10), but first you must decide to take every part as it comes. The journey is awaiting us, are we ready for the challenge? Let me warn you. Once you surrender the "destination driven" way of living, your life will never be the same. And the voice you've been longing to hear and the God you've been aching to know will be found by you - on the way. So hold on tight, this ride's going to be good!

POPPING THE QUESTIONS:

1. On a scale of 1-10, 1 being Destination Driven and 10 being Journey Focused, how would you rate yourself?

2. Ask someone you trust to answer this question – Am I Destination Driven or Journey Focused?

3. What are you risking if you stay Destination Driven and what are the possible rewards if you change?

4. Have you ever missed something because you we're too busy? How did you feel when you realized what you had lost?

5. How does Jesus example of capturing the "on the way" moments encourage you to live?

6. What stands in your way of becoming more Journey Focused? How can you change?

TRAVEL SHOTS – GETTING READY FOR THE TRIP OF A LIFETIME

Are you destination driven? Perhaps now you're ready to admit it. Or maybe you just "know this friend" that suffers from the illness. As with any disease, the first step in finding a cure is making the correct diagnosis.

In the interest of science and the advancement of treating such a disorder, I've devised a little test to expose our view of life. The purpose is to probe deep beneath our perfect and polished exteriors to the "destination self" lying within. These questions examine what we deem important, a good start to discovering the cure. Let me caution you to answer carefully. Only honest answers produce results accurate enough to assess your condition. Are you ready? Here we go ...

1. Do you prefer fast food because you like it or because you don't have to sit down?
2. At the check out counter do you jump back and forth between lines trying to get the quickest checker (or at least think about doing it)?
3. When your flight is delayed does your temper soar?

4. When attending your kids' recital do you sit back and relax or glance at your watch every few minutes hoping you won't miss the news?

5. When the church service goes into overtime do you go into critical (of the) mass?

6. Does the very mention of the word "shopping" cause you anxiety?

7. When someone makes a mistake is your patience a virtue or an extinct species?

8. When faced with rude or slow drivers does your Christian verbiage transform from blessing to cursing?

9. Do you really want to know the answer to the question, "How are you doing?"

10. Do you eat with your family or with the TV?

11. Does it take a vacation from your vacation to get you to relax?

12. When your spouse wants to talk, do you time it?

13. When your schedule is interrupted do you erupt (on the inside)?

14. When reading a book do you skip to the end? (Don't you dare!)

15. When someone asks about you, do you tell them what you do or whom you love?

16. Have you already lost your patience with this chapter because there are too many questions to answer? (COME BACK!)

Well, how did you do? That bad, huh? Don't worry, there's still hope for us. Don't be discouraged by your affliction, there is a cure. Now you might want to know whether you passed the test or at least beat the national average. I won't tell you. If you *really* need to know, I'll let you in on a little secret - your drivenness is showing.

You may be thinking, *"I don't have time for the questions, just give me the answers!"* But a quick fix is neither possible nor beneficial for what ails the destination driven. I hate to be the one to drop the bomb, but the cure takes time. Remember this is the journey of a lifetime. The priorities and focus we've shaped and molded over years won't magically transform over night. Change will come, but only as we are willing to take the time – to live on the way. But first we need to take our medicine.

IT'S MEDICATION TIME!

A few years back I was bequeathed the "privilege" of taking my son for his pre-school shots (actually I just drew the short straw – but I never did get to see the one my wife had). Arriving on time for this wonderful occasion, we were escorted to a pint size examination room. The nurse walked in cradling a cold metal tray, three syringes lay on the polished surface. Both my son and I fidgeted in discomfort. This didn't look good.

She asked Will to remove his pants and then requested my help. "OK dad," she began, "I need you to hold him down while I commence with the procedure." *Hold him down! Are you crazy? Restrain my precious son while you stick daggers into his leg?*

I will never forget the look on his face as I held his shaking form and the nurse punctured his thigh. I could see the hurt, feel the sense of betrayal – his little eyes welled with tears as the pain spread across his face. Finally the last shot released its contents, leaving my son quivering, and my nerves shot.

The nurse told Will how brave he was — *he* was. The doctor entered moments later, the dirty work done, and awarded my son with a free pizza coupon and a comic book. My wife and I marked his courage with a trip to the toy store – a shameless attempt at bribery and hopeful forgiveness.

I did not enjoy that experience - neither did Will. But to prevent him from becoming sick from all the various bugs and viruses he would encounter in his scholastic travels, his shots were essential. And so are ours.

Unlike the doctor who wants to reassure you that what he is about to do won't hurt — when he knows that it will — I'm going to tell you the truth. There is a cure for what ails the Destination Driven, but it's going to sting. And for some of us this is really going to hurt. So roll up your sleeve and close your eyes, I hear the doctor coming now. Jesus Christ has a special dose just for you.

THE SLOW DOWN ELIXIR

Someone once said, "If the devil can't make you bad, he'll make you busy." Many are pulled to run faster than they are able, to frantically spread themselves in more directions and accomplish more goals than reasonably possible.

Jesus told us, "The thief comes to kill, steal, and destroy" (John 10:10). A frantic pace makes for a freaked out person. By providing too much on our proverbial plates, the devil can kill our joy, rob us of peace, and corrode relationships. When we succumb to the temptation of over commitment and out of balance living, we fail to see life's potential and only see its problems. The remedy, perhaps, as Lily Tomlin suggests, "for fast acting relief, try slowing down."[8]

"The archenemy of spiritual authenticity is busyness"
— Bill Hybels from his book Too Busy Not To Pray

JESUS ... ON THE SLOW

For a man with a mission and a purpose, Jesus never seemed to be in a hurry. Even when something urgent popped into his schedule, he didn't rush. John chapter 11 illustrates this fact.

After hearing that Lazarus might die, Jesus' response is a little odd. He does nothing. In fact he waits two whole days before setting off to see his friend.

What held such importance to keep Jesus from "the one he loved?" What ranked higher in priority then saving the life of a friend? Perhaps he's hanging out with his disciples involved in important — guy stuff. Maybe Jesus is teaching them the finer points of rock climbing or talking about the spiritual implications of football.

But didn't Jesus come to save? Wasn't that his mission? So why not rush off to Bethany and do some saving? Why? Because the Messiah wasn't in a hurry, he was in control. His life would be lived out at God's pace, not by man's emergencies. His journey must be savored, even at the expense of the urgent.

Put yourself in Jesus' shoes. What would you have done? I would have rushed off and taken care of Lazarus - maybe even call on the Father to zap me there like lightning. But not Jesus. Life would be taken one step at a time. Nothing along his journey would be missed. God was glorified and Lazarus resurrected only because Jesus was willing to slow down and enjoy the process.

A CRASH COURSE IN SLOWING DOWN

How do we slow down when everything around us is already going so fast? How do we maintain such calm in the jam-packed-days of our lives?

Hit the Brakes! Change isn't easy but it requires that we stop. I know it sounds radical, but we destination driven are radical people. For years we've raced at frantic speeds, driven by our destination — missing much on the way. Slowing up requires the same serious and stubborn tenacity employed in keeping up.

Take a step back and evaluate your pace. Look at your current acceleration toward extermination. Open your heart and mind to hear from God and others. But that takes time, and to give it, you need to stop.

Park it or Pass it! Stopping provides an opportunity to examine our time commitments. Here we can choose what must be accomplished, what can wait, and what needs to be scratched all together. Some tasks need to be "parked"- we just don't have the time for them right now. The cost of trying to make them happen is too great so we need to wait. There is a right time and a right place. Others need to be "passed," they're important but they are not ours to accomplish. There are many good things we can do. In fact there are more good thing that can be done than we have time for. But what are the "God things," what is it that God has for you? It's OK to put something on hold. Even in the midst of the urgent, Jesus waited - he knew God had a right time for Lazarus.

Test Drive a New Word! It's magical on impacting over-committed schedules. You may have heard it as a child. You might use its final tone on your own offspring. The word is, "NO." Test it out for a minute. Notice the effectiveness of these two letters, combined in just the right way. You're asked to do something and you know you're over booked - your family is looking forward to time with you but your boss wants overtime — say it, "NO!"

Using this word may cause some to become angry, but don't take their guilt trip. You have your own journey to concentrate on. Too often we say no to the wrong requests. Whenever we answer yes to one thing we also say no to another. So use both of these words, just make sure to use them correctly — to the right questions. Your true priorities are revealed by which word you choose.

Make Daily Pit Stop! To gain the abundant life requires that we take daily moments to enjoy each day. There's nothing wrong with doing nothing for a few minutes – in fact it's quite refreshing. I'm not advocating laziness or misusing your time. Taking a cat nap when you should be working is not giving God or your employer your best. But most work places have required breaks, and for good reason.

Have you ever noticed how tiring a vacation can be? How many times have you heard from one who comes back from a get-a-way, "I need a vacation from my vacation?" Then there is the epidemic of sickness that hits when ever over-worked and burnt-out people finally do take a break. Why is that? Let me suggest, a few weeks away from the daily grind can't make up for all the pressure we've put our bodies through the other 48 or so weeks of the year. We need more than that. We need consistent pit stops to make sure the pressure doesn't build

I recently heard on the radio of a discovery made by students at Purdue University. The report gave the reason why some popcorn kernels don't pop. Apparently, the unpoppable kernels possessed microscopic holes that released heat and moisture. We can learn a lot from a few unpopped kernels. Let the pressure out a little at a time, and you won't pop.

> *"The trouble with the rat race is that even if you win,*
> *you're still a rat." – Lily Tomlin*[9]

I hear your frustration, "But you don't know my line of work! You don't work for my boss! I'm just too busy to slow down!" And you're right — I don't know — but I do know this. We all have a choice. My job is important, but is it any more important than Christ's? My situation may be critical, but is it more urgent than Lazarus'? No matter what my agenda holds or how full my schedule is, I always have a choice. There's always time to take the medicine. Jesus did, and it turned out pretty good for him.

THE PAY CLOSER ATTENTION PILL

Has someone ever tried to tell you something but you were too distracted to pay attention? Communication is a difficult thing to master. With all the noise and clutter in life we struggle with being understood and understanding others. Try watching a game on TV as someone attempts to share important information. This can lead to all sorts of deluded stories and disruptive situations.

It was Saturday, and Saturday is *my* day to watch College Football. One such weekend my wife informed me that my lunch was in the oven and she was headed out for a long day of shopping. To be honest, she could have told me our sonl was being eaten by a lion and I wouldn't have heard her. "That's nice honey," was my distracted reply. It's understandable. It was 4th and 1. This was no ordinary game - this was my team, locked in mortal combat with a hated cross-state rival. The climactic moment of tension was my only focus. Captured by the television, I missed the important facts about my meal. Yet it's amazing how effective the squealing sounds of the smoke detector can be.

Jarred into reality by the blaring sound of pending disaster, I emerged from my football induced comatose. Awareness slowly drifted back ... much like the cloud of smoke from the kitchen. As I attempted to rescue my lunch a thought occurred to me — I should have paid closer attention. I don't remember who won that game — but I will never forget the mess made by my neglect. A few charred French fries and burnt fish sticks matter little compared to the more devastating alarms and losses that can be created when we don't pay attention along life's journey.

JESUS ... AT ATTENTION

The teachings of Jesus reveal a man who paid close attention to the world around him. "Look at the lilies of the field and the sparrows of the air," he taught, as he reminded us not to worry (Matthew 5:26-28). He used a parable about seed and soil and their ability to make things grow to describe the power of the Word in the hearts of men (Matthew 13:3).

Jesus once asked, "Have you ever noticed the tiny mustard seed?" He wanted to show us how the kingdom of God would start small but branch out to fill the world (Matthew 13:31). Jesus identified believers as branches and called himself the vine, illustrating our relationship to him – describing the flow of spiritual life and ministry that comes from intimacy with God (John 15). He connected with people through common observations – ordinary examples they personally experienced.

Jesus was an expert at discovery. He saw the Samaritan woman at the well and entered her life - perceiving both her words and what hid beneath them. He heard the cries of blind Bartimaeus. He felt the loneliness as he touched the unclean leper. He recognized the diminutive tax collector, Zacchaeus, sitting in a tree.

Jesus bent to write a message in the sand to save the life of one caught in adultery. Even in his agony on the cross, he heard the cries of a condemned thief at his side and offered paradise. He looked at Jerusalem and saw the ripe harvest, hoping his disciples might see the same, that they might pay attention.

And just look at the motley crew he chose - living proof that Jesus was an expert at seeing something in people that evaded others.

I've heard parents say of their children's troubles, "I just didn't see it coming." Marriages fall apart because, "She just stopped noticing me." The workaholic husband convinces himself, "But I'm doing it for them." The absent son laments, "I thought Dad would be around forever."

My little boy often strives to gain my attention with the phrase, "Daddy look!" or, "Daddy, do you know what?" Once I was so into my own world he used the only name he knew would rattle me, "Pastor Rick," he shouted. To be completely honest it's not always convenient to stop. Will grabs my attention with the earth shaking news that he wants to be a pirate at the church harvest party, but it's July. He startles me with the proclamation that he wants a castle for his birthday, but he was born in June and it's not yet December. I stop and listen – most of the time.

But why should I? Why should my important projects be set aside for a child's dreams? Why waste time to pay attention to the relatively insignificant? Because someday he might stop asking - someday I may be the one begging for his attention. And if I don't give it now I won't get it later.

THE FORMULA FOR PAYING ATTENTION

Paying attention requires three scarce resources– time, careful observation, and the commitment to listen. Only by combining these three ingredients can we harness the full power of the prescribed remedy.

Time is the most crucial component in becoming journey focused. We need time to see and hear what is happening around us. Without a sacrifice of our time the people in our lives will never feel important. No matter how much we give or do for them, love will go unaccepted. Because we weren't there to give it. Likewise we must allow ourselves time to change, and request grace from others as we commit to becoming active observers. This leads to the second step.

Though we try, often we lack the ability to *carefully observe* the ones closest to us. To pay attention requires our powers of observation. Good intentions have little value, if they are not followed by active participation.

If my wife does something new to herself, goes to work and hears all day long from her girlfriends and co-workers how nice her hair looks or how stunning her new outfit is, then returns home and I don't notice? Well let's just say I've learned to pay attention.

"Somebody is going to feel as if I am not giving them what they deserve or need, the issue is always, 'Where (or

who) am I choosing to cheat?'" — Andy Stanley from his
book <u>Choosing to Cheat</u>

The commitment to pay attention continues with the ***undivided investment to listen***. James, the brother of Jesus, wrote, *"Be quick to listen."*(James 1:19). Listeners, willing to give of their time, are in short supply. This rare breed makes valuable friends because they value others, demonstrating this through their listening.

One of the greatest road blocks to marital bliss is poor communication. Even when something else seems the more obvious culprit, bad communication nearly always gnaws at the root.

As a pastor I counsel pre-marriage couples on a variety of issues. One of the steepest challenges comes from teaching active listening skills. Through eye contact and paraphrasing what the other is saying couples learn to communicate more effectively.

Many conversations are one person listening to half of what is said, then as the "speaker" continues the "listener" starts to formulate a response. How often do we really hear everything that the other is trying to say? Let alone catch what is not said in body language, facial expressions, and voice tone.

After one such session I came home to my wife and realized something. The very skill I had just promoted to the bride and groom-to-be went unused by "the counselor" at home. I think Tamara knows when I'm doing pre-marital counseling; I tend to be a better listener.

In any relationship whether employer-employee, parent-child, husband-wife, or any other involving human contact (and sometimes pets too), try adding a touch more listening and a little less advice — observe its impact. I guarantee it will help; decreasing the occurrence of charred food and relationship burn out.

THE PUPOSE FOCUSED NOT GOAL DRIVEN SERUM

A cartoon once adorned my office wall that read, "I was put on this planet to accomplish a certain number of tasks ... I am so far behind right now that I'll never die." Now that's a rough way to gain immortality.

This last dose of medication causes difficulties for the "task oriented." Those who live for goals fulfilled and quotas met choke a little when trying to swallow the thick liquid that makes up this concoction. Yet, to assure a full recovering we must force it down.

How do goals and purpose differ? I offer a few thoughts. Goals are concrete measuring sticks, tools to help us arrive at some point or destination. Goals are time bound, number based targets - tasks to accomplish. All goals end in success or failure, but they all end. The greatest danger comes when we give goals too much power. As masters, goals make us unbalanced – driven to achieve at any cost. When numbers hold the higher priority, the ends justify the means.

In contrast, purpose strives to maintain balance. How you get there is just as important as getting there. Purpose is not accomplished – it's too big for that – it is lived out, day by day, moment by moment. Goals are numbers we shoot for, purpose is the reason we live for. Purpose is why I exist, why I get up in the morning, why I press on even after the goal is gone. Whether my goal ends in failure or success my purpose lives on.

Even "good" goals can drive us away from our purpose. Ministry goals are good, yet to neglect your purpose as a spouse, sibling, or parent to attain them is self-defeating. Becoming debt free is admirable, but not in exchange for time with God and his people – this accrues eternal deficits. Success tastes wonderful, but ignoring the needs of others will produce awards without substance. Goals are useful, but not at the expense of life. They must not drive us past our purpose.

A Side Note - Food for Thought

The Bible is full of numbers. The Gospels describe crowds of people, money, and even fish by their size and quantity. Yet at no point does Jesus ever sit down and set a concrete numerical goal with his disciples. Numbers merely reported the results of a life of purpose. In the Book of Acts, the number of believers grew, not as they aimed to meet goals, but rather as they lived out purpose. When taken to the extreme, trading goals for purpose borders on idolatry. Jesus did not set out to meet a quota, he was sent to save the world.

JESUS' CHOICE … PURPOSE OR GOALS?

Jesus was a man of purpose. His goals were clear yet his purpose to love mankind came first - impacting his treatment of everyone, even the insignificant.

"Choosy moms choose Jiff," a peanut butter commercial declares. With the Messiah around, smart parents wasted little time on this bread spread. Choosy parents brought their children to Jesus.

But when they found him they met with resistance. The planning committee, made up of Jesus' disciples, told the families to go away. In their goal-driven state of mind they found little purpose for these intruders. "Get these snot nosed kids out of the way …. This is Jesus the Christ. His appointment book is full." Overhearing this, Jesus rebuked his disciples, "Let the little children come to me and do not hinder them, for such is the kingdom of God." (Matthew 19:14)

To Jesus life was not goals, it was the kingdom. Because his purpose drove him, rather than accomplishing a set order of tasks, he had plenty of time for anyone who wanted to seek him. He saw them not as intruders but as invited. If only his disciples today could see those who do not fit in the same way. Intrusions become special guests when we focus on purpose and not goals.

KEEPING THE PURPOSE STRAIGHT

The destination driven often exchange goals for purpose, finding them cheap substitutes and poor counterfeits. Only journey-men, focused on purpose, capture the treasure found on the way. The obvious question proceeds, what is our purpose?

Using a seventeenth century creed, John Piper proposes, "The chief end (purpose) of man is to glorify God by enjoying him forever."[10] In his book *It's Not About Me,* Max Lucado suggests, "Reduce the human job description down to one phrase, and this is it: Reflect God's glory … God sends the message; we mirror it." *In The Purpose Driven Life*, Pastor Rick Warren condenses our purpose into five key words: worship, fellowship, discipleship, ministry, and evangelism. I like Steve Farrar's mission statement – "Don't screw up."[11] Wow, we've come a long way since, "Be fruitful and multiply." So who's right? Let's ask Jesus.

Since the days of Christ to now, our purpose really hasn't changed all that much. Through the passing of time, the evolving of cultures, and the sky rocketing of technology, the reason for our existence remains constant. Love.

A Pharisee once asked Jesus which commandment stood above the rest. Jesus' answer reveals our purpose. "Love the Lord your God with all your heart and with all your soul and with all your mind ... and love your neighbor as yourself. All the Law and the Prophets hang on these two commands" (Matthew 22:37-40). Mark and Luke both record similar discussions, stressing the importance of this answer.

Our purpose can be boiled down to one statement – love God and love others. That seems a little general, yet it is the broad scope which releases the beauty. Our purpose is not a task or goal to be accomplished. It is an adventure to be lived out. The Apostle Paul plotted our coarse, "find out what pleases God" (Ephesians 5:10).

The unique quality of Christianity is that it is not "religion based" but relationship based. Love holds sway over our choices and purpose, not law. To be a Christian is to be a traveler — to pack up and prepare to take a journey with God — following in the footsteps of his Son. To love God and others is a process of discovery and faith. Learning what fulfills these commands then living them out is our reason for being.

To learn more about your purpose, I suggest another book. This volume stands alone atop the all-time best sellers list. In fact you probably own one already – the Bible. It remains the finest authority on the subject, and the only fool proof text available. The authors quoted above stand on solid ground because their answers grew from the fertile soil of God's Word. "As for God his way is perfect; the word of the Lord is flawless." (II Samuel 22:31)

It might be easier if I just spelled it out for you. But where is the fun in that? Besides, that would defeat ... the purpose.

Is the medicine going down? Are you seeing life in a new light? If not, don't worry, like most medication it takes time – and a commitment to be faithful with the dosage. You <u>can</u> slow down, you <u>can</u> pay attention, and you <u>can</u> live by purpose for, "He who began a good work in you *will* carry it on to completion" (Philippians 1:6).

MEDITATING ON THE MEDICATION:

1. How often do you slow down? What keeps you from slowing down? What are some things you do to slow down?

2. How well do you pay attention? What distracts you from paying attention? How can you better your abilities to pay attention?

3. What is the difference between goals and purpose? Why is it important to be purpose focused and not goal driven? Have your choices or actions ever shown that goals were more important than people?

4. Who are you cheating of your time, energy and attention? If you don't like your answer, how will you begin change this week?

5. How does Jesus' ability to slow down, pay attention, and live purpose focused impact you?

Stop #3

"IS THE JOURNEY REALLY NECESSARY?"—THE HIGHWAY OF HUMILITY AND TESTING

Being a kid and going to the movies. I loved it. I can still remember standing outside the movie theatre in downtown Seattle awaiting the 1977 release of the original Star Wars movie. The line was enormous and the wait seemed endless, but that night triggered in me a youthful fascination with science fiction. One that lingers still today.

In the summer of 2005 I took my own son to see the final Star Wars movie. The clash of electric sabers stirred his imagination just as they had captured mine nearly 30 years ago. The possibility of new places and strange faces; to think beyond our small world to another and to ponder the possibilities of becoming a space exploring, weapon wielding hero ... that was excitement.

But for me, the most intriguing facet of science fiction is the "speed"... Jumping to light speed, pushing the warp engines, and traveling so fast that you could actually go back in time. That was cool! But best of all I was fascinated by the technology which allowed a person to be "transported." For those, not educated in the finer points of space travel, let me explain.

The theory of transportation goes something like this: *The transporter device converts objects or persons into energy. That energy is then sent to a desired destination and reconstructed in that new location. The transporter reconstitutes the object or person from energy back into matter.*[12] All of this in just a matter of seconds. (Actually God came up with the idea first – See Genesis 5:24, and Acts 8:39)

All this speed made me want to get to my destination; causing me to ask the question, *"Is the Journey REALLY Necessary?"* The next three chapters provide a glimpse at why the answer to this question is a resounding YES!

> *"God isn't going to let you see the distant scene. So you might as well quit looking for it. He promises a lamp unto our feet, not a crystal ball into our future. We do not need to know what will happen tomorrow. We only need to know he leads us and 'we will find grace to help us when we need it' (Heb. 4:16 NLT)"* — *Max Lucado from his book Traveling Light*

JOINING MOSES AT THE EDGE OF THE PROMISED LAND

Journeys are often exciting but rarely easy. At first, evaluating life in the context of the journey may seem rather pleasant; flowery expressions, poetic metaphors, roadway imagery, with a touch of "other worldliness" conjuring visionary ideas and whimsical emotions. Then the clouds roll in and the real journey takes shape.

When faced with the realities of life, the prospect of the process loses much of its appeal. Tough times, dreams dashed, relationships ruined, finances failing, health harpooned and all of a sudden we say, "You can keep the journey, Lord, just beam me up … or at least out of this mess!"

Perhaps Moses and the Israelites felt the same way in their wandering through the wilderness. For forty years God led them on a highway through the desert in order to deal with their deficiencies. But that time had come and gone; now they were ready to claim the promise.

Moses stood before the people. Looking across the vast sea of faces he reminded them of the reasons God sent them into the dessert "death march" that cost the lives of an entire generation. They could not afford to let their experiences go to waste. It was crucial that the lessons learned in the desert journey be taken into the process of the conquest.

But the insight they gained is not just faded history, it is available for us to utilize in our own travels as well. The Apostle Paul instructed, "Now these things occurred as examples to keep us from setting our hearts on evil things as they did ... These things happened to them as examples and were written down as warnings for us on whom the fulfillment of the ages has come." (1 Corinthians 10:6 and 11)

Their stumbling and bumbling has been recorded, not solely for our entertainment or for their embarrassment, but that we might avoid the bad choices and hard lessons that plagued their journey.

Follow me back in time to that spot near the valley of Beth Peor, the gateway into Canaan, to Moses last days with his people. It is here we begin to understand why the Journey is really necessary; to fry pride, reveal our character, and protect our future.

The Journey Comes that Pride Might Go ... To Humble Our Self-Sufficiency

Charles Swindoll tells a story of a wonderfully humble man of God. It seems this Pastor was unanimously voted by his congregation as the most humble pastor in America. In appreciation and to recognize this admirable quality in their shepherd the church gave him a medal which was engraved with the words, "To the most humble pastor in America." Well it didn't last long. They promptly took it away from him the next Sunday when he wore it.[13]

"Humility is a strange thing. The minute you think you've got it, you've lost it." E. D. Hulse[14]

God saw this same pride in his people as they approached the land of Canaan. Once slaves to a ruthless Egyptian task master, now freedom released the monster that lay dormant in their hearts. Whipped and chained no more, pride rose to find expression against the very God who set them free. Once aroused it took control.

Pride doesn't die easily. And most often its extermination only happens in the deserts of life; there in the wastelands it can be starved and brought low. For nearly half a century the Israelites were reminded of the pain and suffering that pride brings into the lives of those it touches. The price is high; it cost the Children of Israel 40 years and an entire generation, living proof of the words of Solomon, "Pride goes before destruction and a haughty spirit before a fall." (Proverbs 16:18)

In the wilderness God set out to humble his people. Before entering the Promise Land, Moses reminded them of their need for humility. "Remember how the LORD your God led you all the way in the desert these forty years, to humble you … He gave you manna to eat in the desert, something your fathers had never known, to humble (you)…" (Deuteronomy 8:2 and 16)

How could God's provision humble His people? How could having your needs met bruise your pride? Well, maybe you've never had to depend on the generosity of others to survive. My wife and I have experienced such times in our lives; resources low, responsibilities high. As the saying goes, "We had more month than we had money"

In our first few months of marriage, I was in a car accident that cost my job. If you know anything about newlyweds most possess little. So when most of your little is lost, so are you. But somehow, some way all the bills were paid. No one gave us the money, and I can't quite explain it, but when the bills came the money was there. Through the love and care of God's people we had more food during that time than any time before or since.

This has happened several times during our ministry; tires provided, doctor bills paid for, cars repaired for free, empty freezers filled. But I will tell you this, it is a humbling thing. To admit your need and receive help from others pricks a decisive hole through the balloon of pride and self-suffiency.

This is the humility God chose to teach the Israelites, a humility that would lead them to trust Him. Like children clinging to the hand of a parent, "God led them all the way ... for forty years."(Deuteronomy 8:2) It is a humbling thing to be led by the hand, but in life it is the only certain way to make it Home. God humbles us that we might let go of our desire for control.

Many times my young son insists, "I can do it myself, Daddy!" We often say the same thing to God. But trust and pride cannot coexist in the same heart (see Proverbs 28:25).

The Apostle Paul wrote, "My God shall supply all your needs, according to his riches in glory." (Philippians 4:19). His riches, not yours. The Prophet Jeremiah wrote, "Cursed is he who trusts in the arm of the flesh." (Jeremiah 17:5). Only in the journey do we learn that our own strength is too weak to save.

Why does it seem that so many come to Jesus in times of crisis? Why pray when bad things happen? Because the Journey has a way of humbling us and exposing our weaknesses and inadequacies.

> *"Humility is the foundation for all the other virtues;*
> *hence, in the soul in which this virtue does not exist there*
> *cannot be any other virtue except in mere appearance."*
> *St. Augustine[15]*

HUMBLE ENOUGH TO RECEIVE

For the Israelites over 400 years of slavery broke into new-found freedom. Knowing only a life of abuse and restriction, they now experienced wide open places, promise, and possibilities. Yet after such a long period of time in captivity the Israelites grew hard and untrusting. They had learned to survive by keeping closed off, depending upon themselves. But this new life demanded a change – they must understand their need for help.

With our new found gift of humility we recognize an important fact for of the journey. I can't do this alone.

My father in law is a huge fan of western books. Louie Lamore has a sacred place in his collection of over 40 years of religious books, sermons, and Bible reference works.

Have you ever noticed how often western heroes need a hero? You've seen it. The inevitable show down is about to begin. The streets of the town are quickly cleared as all the towns' folk scurry inside like frightened mice. The shop owners board up the windows and put up the closed sign (As if that act would somehow protect the glass).

A lone tumble weed blows across main street, and as always, one lone business remains open; the saloon. A smallish, yet over-weight bartender methodically wipes out a shot glass and places it on the table, just as our hero walks in and says, "Fill it up ... and leave the bottle."

All is quiet. All is still. But it won't be that way for long. After a dramatic pause and a little more sarsaparilla (of course, real heroes don't drink whiskey), a voice of challenge shatters the tranquility. From the street the villain issues an insult laced proposition; the battle is about to begin.

What ensues is a gunfight for the ages, covering the entire town. Back and forth their six shooters blaze firing off endless shots – without reloading. Somehow they've managed to miss each other and at the same time shatter every window in town. Finally through obvious trickery and dubious cheating the villain gets the drop on our hero. Though not a mortal wound, this cowboy's gun is out of reach as the villain slowly approaches. Clink, clink, clink.

Like all evil doers, a simple shot to the head is not enough. He breaks into a brief monologue taunting his wounded adversary. And of course his speech becomes his undoing.

A moment before the dastardly deviant pulls the trigger another shot is heard. The villain drops. Behind him a woman steps out, smoking shot gun poised where the man in black once stood. Of course, she will marry our hero and live happily ever after.

No matter how talented, wise, or strong a hero we may be, at one point we all need help. We need each other. *Understand this; the humbling process is for our benefit.* Without humility most would never make it to the destination. We learn this in the journey, on the Highway of Humility. A very good reason why the journey *is REALLY* necessary.

WHY DO WE NEED HUMILITY?

Still having difficulty understanding why humility is so important? Here is a quick list of reason that Bible gives us for the essential need to destroy pride and self-sufficiency in our lives.

Humility is the prelude to Honor. "Humility comes before
honor." (Proverbs 15:33). Jesus echoed these words, "For whoever
exalts himself will be humbled, and whoever humbles himself will
be exalted" (Matthew 23:12). Scripture teaches that the only way to
find honor is to serve others, the only way to be lifted up is to take a
seat. (See also Job 5:11, Luke 1:52, James 4:10, 1 Peter 5:6)

Theirs is the Kingdom. "Blessed are the poor in spirit for theirs is
the Kingdom of heaven ... Blessed are the meek for they shall inherit
the earth" (Matthew 5:3, 5). The true Lords of the earth and heirs of
heaven are those who conquer their own pride not those who subdue
nations.

Your place in the Kingdom. A deciding factor of how we will
live in our eternal home, "... white washed tombs with dead men's
bones inside" (Matthew 23:27), is our level of humility. "Whoever
humbles himself like this little child is the greatest in the Kingdom
of Heaven." (See Matthew 18:2-4)

Forgiveness found, grace gained. The contrite tax collector, not
the arrogant Pharisee received forgiveness (See Luke 18:9-14) and
went away justified. James and Peter both wrote, "God opposes the
proud but gives grace to the humble." (James 4:6 and I Peter 5:5).

God is Near. An intimate relationship with God only grows in
the fertile soil of humility. "I live with him who is contrite and lowly
in spirit." (Isaiah 57:15)

The Way to Wisdom belongs to the teachable. "With humility
comes wisdom." (Proverbs 11:2). Experts think themselves wise
because they know. Students think themselves wise because they
learn. But wisdom is found by those who walk in humility, pliable in
God's hands. He reveals his wisdom to children and to those whom
the world considers foolish (See Luke 10:21 and 1 Corinthians
1:27)

The Cost is too high without it. There is a cost for side stepping the process of humility. The Lord warned Israel, "Then your

heart will become *proud* and you will *forget* the LORD your God … If you ever *forget* the LORD … you will surely be destroyed." (Deuteronomy 8:14, 19 emphasis mine) God knows that if He uses us before He humbles us we will fall into the same trap as the Devil, supplanting God on the throne and taking His glory. (See 1 Timothy 3:6)

THE JOURNEY COMES TO TEST OUR QUALITY

Two minerals look amazingly similar yet their worth is worlds apart. To the untrained eye they differ little, but test them with fire and their value is revealed. One is priceless, the other pyrite. A truck load of the first would secure your financial future, the other just colorful gravel. The test reveals everything, whether we are fool's gold, or the real thing.

If our lives were tested would we find pure gold or worthless pyrite? The journey is necessary because it tests our value. Only through the process are we weighed and measured to see what lies within; true value or just a good show. The unfortunate discovery comes when we resemble the Pharisees of Jesus' time

It's not the performance that matters; it is the private; not the perceived illusion of godly living, but the practical daily application. God wants us to find out what we're made of and where we're headed before it's too late

"A smooth sea never made a skillful sailor" – Unknown[16]

In the wilderness God tested His people to uncover their character. "Remember how the LORD your God led you all the way in the desert these forty years, to humble you and *to test* you in order to know what was in your heart..." (Deuteronomy 8:2)

Nothing tests our character like a journey … Destinations often let us relax and kick back; after all we've "arrived." There is little pressure or stress once we accomplish our goal and achieve our objective. But in the process we really get to see what we are made of.

A television show, which dedicated itself to the high calling of making others look bad, once replaced the normal contents of a toothpaste tube with raw hamburger meat. You can image the reaction of those expecting minty freshness when they received a mouth full of yesterday's ground beef. For some it was a wakeup call and for others a call for the nearest garbage can.

The aftermath of pressure is a great indicator of our character. When we get squeezed we witness what comes out, and so does God. The journey lets us uncover our character and, better still, do something about it.

On the way to Capernaum, Jesus' disciples got into a bit of an argument. When they arrived at their destination Jesus asked what their "intense fellowship" was all about.

What might stir such strong emotions among these future church pillars? How to reach the lost sheep of Israel? No. How they might help the poor in the next town? No. The great teachings of their master? Perhaps the transfiguration that Peter, James, and John just witnessed? Maybe the healing of the demon-possessed boy in the last village? No, No, No. These spiritual giants were having a flexing contest.

The disciples were arguing about who was the greatest. With all the needs and all the power and all the amazing experiences around them these guys are doing an "I'm-better-than-you" debate (See Mark 9). Of course Jesus directs them to true greatness, but just as important they learned how completely "un-great" they really were. Their hearts were revealed, their pride was exposed, and their character fell far short. They had been tested — on the way— and learned they had a long way to go.

GUARD OUR FUTURE

Without the tests of the past there would be no future. God knew his people would falter and doubt. At times, the Israelites deserved to be rejected, as do we, but God's covenant remained unbreakable; he was in for the long haul. So he sent them into the barren wastelands to protect them, to guard their future. "He gave you manna to eat in the desert, something your fathers had never known, to

humble and to test you so that *in the end* it might go well with you."
(Deuteronomy 8:16, emphasis mine).

God knows the only way the story of our lives will "go well" is
if we're tested. The little, gradual tests at the beginning prepare us
for what's ahead. Even if the process is slow and time consuming
we will be grateful for the first steps when facing the mountainous
ones.

Do you remember how stressed out and burdened certain tasks
once made you feel? How overwhelming some responsibilities were
when you first faced them? Have you also noticed how many of
those things don't even faze you anymore? That's the protection I'm
speaking of. God guards our future by forcing us to grow now.

I didn't want to do it, but I knew the day would come. I dreaded
it, ignored it, but I could not avoid it. The diving board mocked my
fear and heightened my apprehension. Every week I went to the
pool, relieved that today had not been *THE DAY*.

My perseverance found strength in the form of my knock dead
gorgeous swimming instructor. Yet even her entrancing beauty could
not stop that diving board from ruining my summer and torturing
my dreams.

But no matter how hard I tried to wish it away, *THE DAY* finally
came. We all lined up behind "the plank" as our beautiful swimming instructor transformed before our young eyes into the merciless Captain Hook. As she prodded us forward toward our watery
doom, my mind went into overdrive. Scared, panicky, and looking
for a way out I faced my turn on the board like a man. I hid in the
bathroom.

For over half an hour I crouched on the cold, wet tile floors,
attempting to avoid the plunge; enduring the uncomfortable comfort
of the familiar bathroom to bypass the unknown.

That little leap off the diving board was nothing compared to the
leaps of faith I've been forced to take since that summer break. To
my never ending shame and disgrace, I never jumped off that board.
I've never become much of a swimmer either.

If we skip the little tests in the journey we will never become
prepared for the bigger ones. Without the small daily examinations,

we are incapable to walk in what those tiny tedious tests were meant to teach us.

Maybe you were born a fish or a natural swimmer, so it's hard to relate to my trials (by the way, you people really hurt my kind with your mockery and jokes, but we forgive you). But each of us faces tests. They may intimidate at first, but they really offer protection.

Aren't you glad when you went to Kindergarten that they didn't start you out in algebra or chemistry? It's probably a good thing. All those chemicals in the hands of 30 five and six year olds could be pretty dangerous. We'd think the teacher cruel and unfair to put poor kindergartners in such a predicament. They need to start small, at the beginning. Give them a few years and they'll be ready to take on the elemental chart and the pellagrous theorem. But not yet, first things first.

Tests are not to cause pain in our present, but rather to protect our tomorrow. The pop quizzes we go through everyday prepare us for the "Final Exam" and protect our Eternal Future! The Heavenly Teacher may feel distant, quiet, and unconcerned during your test, but that's only because he knows you can handle it, that you need it, and is waiting to review the results once it's all over.

GETTING THE MOST OUT OF EVERY TEST

In Order to gain all we can from the tests of life we must prepare. But how can we ready ourselves for the unknown? In the academic world there are hundreds of books promising to prepare students for the scholarly challenges that loom before them. One such book, *Barron's How to Prepare for the CLEP*, provides ten keys to successful test results. As we come to the end of the 3rd stop on our journey I've taken the principles and applied them to the tests we face in life. Who would have guessed that those who prepare well for a CLEP test may have a jump on the rest of us?

> *1. Get plenty of sleep* — When your body is worn out and your mind burnt out your ability to learn and respond diminishes greatly. As one of my college professors said, "sometimes the most spiritual thing we can do is take a nap."

2. *Arrive early* — When we give our body the rest it needs then we are able to give it what it needs most. "Arriving early" to everyday life begins with consistent time alone with God.

3. *Take a watch* — We will fair best against tests when we follow the men of Issachar, "who understood the times and knew what Israel should do." (2 Chronicles 12:32). What are the times you live in? What needs to be done? When we understand this, we are better prepared for the pop quizzes we face.

4. *Wear Comfortable Clothes* — The best suit for the tests we will face is the Armor of God (Ephesians 6:10-17). Putting this ensemble on through prayer and practical obedience will make the tests conquerable and our enemy uncomfortable.

5. *Do not assume anything regarding the directions* — Don't make decisions before consulting divine direction. Life is an open Book test if we'll take advantage of it.

6. *Relax* — "Be anxious for nothing," Paul wrote the Philippians. Tests will come, we can't stop them, but worry helps no one. So relax, pray and allow "the peace of God which passes all understanding" to guard your heart and mind (Philippians 4:6-7). God won't allow a test he knows you cannot pass.

7. *Pace Yourself* — Life is a marathon, not a 100 yard dash. Take everything as it comes. Don't load yourself down with more responsibilities and work while you're experiencing a time of testing.

8. *Read all the choices before choosing, your first answer isn't necessarily the right one* — Gut reactions are often the wrong decisions. Don't just react to the test. Weigh your options, listen to God, and then make a wise and informed choice.

9. *Record Answers Correctly* — When you've learned from the test or heard from God make sure to follow through. Remember: knowing is ONLY half the battle.

10. *Never choose (E)* — In this case (E) stands for Escape. When you face a test don't run from it, you'll only have to face it again later.[17]

The Israelites discovered that God's intentions for their years in the wilderness were to prepare them for the conquest. He needed to mold them to be able to hold on to what they were given. So in his infinite wisdom and love, God sent them into the dessert to humble and to test them; to provide for them the crucible that would place their hope and sufficiency in Him alone —the furnace that would purify their character.

God wants you to make it. He doesn't want ignorance to come back to bite you. So he tests his chosen, "so that in the end it might go well with you."

Take it from one who still can't swim very well. When God tests you don't jump aside or run and hide. The only way to find out who you are and secure your future is to take the test. So when God comes testing, dive in. The waters of the journey are REALLY necessary.

ANSWERS TO THE TEST:

1. Think of a time you were humbled? Is there a difference between God's humbling and another source? Did the event help you or hinder you?

2. How has your character been tested in the past? How might God be testing your character today? What can you learn from the desserts you may be experiencing?

3. What have these situations taught you about yourself and God? How have you become better for them?

4. What have you learned that would benefit others? Who might God put on your heart to share these valuable treasures with?

5. How is God protecting your future with your today? Make a list of past victories and growing spurts God has led you through.

Stop #4

"IS THE JOURNEY REALLY NECESSARY?" – THE PATHWAY OF PRIORITY

" *I can't hold on,*" the thought flashed through his mind even as his grip began to weaken, "*I have to let go of one of them.*" The choice was unavoidable, the consequences unmistakable. Either let go of the girl or the treasure, but holding both was impossible. In a fleeting moment he would decide which meant more. So he let go, his priority revealed … as the girl fell toward the pit below. This scene has been repeated in movies, literature, and even in life. Most recently I witnessed it again while watching the movie *National Treasure*.

Benjamin Gates, a devoted treasure hunter, finds himself clinging to a wooden elevator while the woman he loves grasps his other hand. Staring up toward the loosening planks he discovers his treasure, the Declaration of Independence, precariously nestled on the crumbling platform. Drop the girl or lose the document, which would it be? Of course he dropped the person and held tightly to the possession.[18]

In the journey we face moments – choices – that unveil our priorities. Talk is forced to walk as our actions prove what we truly treasure most. God places our feet on the Pathway of Priority to reveal what we value and to shape those values to mirror his own.

As we revisit the Israelites on the doorstep of Canaan, Moses warns them to remember the cost of forgetting what matters most. As God's people fled Egypt they were haunted by the ghost of mixed up priorities. The rapid transition from four centuries of slavery to freedom left them dazed and confused. They chose the illusion of self, not service. They valued feelings, not following God.

Swords were sharpened, spears made ready, shields and bows prepared for battle, yet there remained the need for another weapon; priority. So Moses reminded his people to not forget the lesson of the wilderness; to know and to keep what matters most.

PRIORITY SHIFT

Before the desert, Israel whined about not having food to eat. Even as they traveled they tested God. He needed to show them physical bread wasn't their greatest concern, rather the bread that feeds the soul. He addressed what they valued most and what they should consider of much greater worth.

"He (God) humbled you, causing you to hunger and then feeding you with manna, which neither you nor your fathers had known, *to teach* you that man does not live on bread alone but on every word that comes from the mouth of the LORD." (Deuteronomy 8:3). With one statement Moses outlined the changes needed in the priorities of his people. In his book *A Passionate Pursuit of God,* Tim Riter comments, "Even with the law God desired not rule keeping but a priority relationship. A relationship we value more than any other – a relationship to which all other pursuits yield." For Israel to have the right priorities four shifts in their thinking would be required.

From Material to Spiritual – As they cried out for physical reprieve the Israelites neglected their spiritual need. Their thoughts we're so focused on getting fed they could not see the amazing opportunity before them.

The God they heard so much about was available, his word alive in their hearts, if only they would receive him. But their growling bellies overcame the deeper need of the Spirit. Today, "the belly" continues to win priority in many Christians' lives. The Apostle Paul wrote of those infatuated with temporary desires, "their God is their stomachs." (Philippians 3:19).

We see our lack and list our wants and at the same time miss the more amazing blessing of knowing God. God is more than an unlimited bank account or guaranteed health plan. He promises to supply all our needs, but what we need isn't just a matter of stuff. What we really need has more to do with what we cannot see, eat, or spend; the intangible blessings of the Spirit.

As long as we value God less than our material needs and wants, the groans of our souls will go unmet as we claim and demand our physical desires above him.

From Temporary to Eternal – The Israelites focused on the here and now; not only for their food but also for their futures. Their hearts were set on the Promised Land, not realizing it was only a precursor to a much larger inheritance, an everlasting kingdom.

I've been asked, "What do you want your life to look like in 5, 10, 20, or 30 years from now? What type of ministry do you want to have? What size congregation, place, or position do you want?" Now, there's nothing wrong with those questions. Except they're all focused on now, on this little segment of time we call life. But I have a bigger future.

The Destination Driven, with goals in mind, often miss the greater goal. So earthly minded we forget the Heavenly reward. We must be careful to not exchange the glories of the temporary for the glories of the eternal. It's a bad trade.

My priority should not consist in numbers that impress, or dreams and goals that make me look good. No, my priority must find expression in impacting eternity. Large churches and bountiful ministries are wonderful. Thriving businesses, advancement and promotions are all great. But what do they really matter if they stop here. Eternity will be my home, and eternity should be where I leave my imprint.

From Urgent to Important – Food was the urgent need, so knowing God could wait. Right now they needed to eat, who had time to pray. Often we live like a fire fighter, waking each day to put out the little fires that pop up around us.

The hectic pace of life coupled with overcommitted schedules, leaves little time for anything else. But if we are to possess the right priorities we must decide what is important and what is urgent. Make sure the important things really do receive priority. Then be willing to make the urgent things wait.

> *"Do you know what your family wants from you more than anything else? 'Love?' you say. That's part of it. But it goes deeper than that they want to feel accepted. In practical terms they want to feel like they are a priority ... It is not enough for them to be your priority. They must feel like it." — Andy Stanley from* <u>*Choosing to Cheat*</u>

From Human Wisdom to Heavenly Wisdom – The wisdom employed by the Israelites did not originate from God. It was self-centered, short-sighted, and problem-focused. Panic is not a spiritual gift, whining is not a form of worship. Human wisdom deals with the senses, Heaven's wisdom the Spirit. The journey brings us countless opportunities to gain wisdom that comes from above. It is our job to capture it.

Solomon wrote wisdom begins with the "fear of the Lord" (Proverbs 1:7), and cannot exist without it. For a greater understanding of wisdom search James 3:13-17. Within these verses you will discover the profound difference between God's wisdom and man's.

PRIORITY CHECK

When asked what is important to each of us we know two things ... The truth and what we want to believe. However good intentions don't change the facts, and mixed up priorities don't improve with denial. There are several ways to discover what we value most, the list below is designed to help us honestly answer the question, "What are my priorities?" Take a look at where your priorities stand. See if you may need to do a little shifting as the Israelites did.

1. *Check book* — Where you spend your cash reveals what you care about most. "Where your treasure, there your heart will be also." (Matthew 6:21)
2. *Calendar* — What is important to you receives your time. When we push one thing aside for another we rank their importance.
3. *Consuming* — What you choose to read, watch, and listen to sheds light on what you deem to be important. We value what we consume.
4. *Conversations* — What I talk about matters to me for, "out of the overflow of the heart the mouth speaks." (Matthew 12:34)
5. *Convictions* — Everyone has "pet peeves" and non-negotiables; those issues that they are passionate about and hold strong opinions toward. That which stirs your passions is important to you.
6. *Commitments* — Long term commitments show priority. Memberships, matrimony, and mortgages are a few commitments that require a lifetime and expose what matters to us.
7. *Character* — Your character strengths and weaknesses reveal priority. What you are willing to allow to remain weak is less important. Those character traits you diligently work on changing you hold in higher priority
8. *Compassion* — What moves you emotionally? What moves you to tears? When the chord strings of our hearts are played the tune reveals what we truly care about.

MAKING PRIORITIES STICK

The Journey teaches us priority, but keeping them straight is another issue all together. When I first began writing this book my son had just started Kindergarten. Most of the school work happened at school, with little if any effort on my part. Today my son is in the 4th grade. Much has changed since those early play school days. Where once homework was practically non-existent, now it has become a nightly priority, and sometimes even a trial and test of my patience. I realize some of you are thinking, Just wait till he gets in

Junior High or High School, but as I spoke of earlier, I need the test of 4th grade so I can survive those days to come.

Will's journey has taught us both that if he is going to continue his climb up the academic food chain homework must be a priority. And that works just fine in the dead of a cold Montana winter. But add a little sunshine, witness the snow melt away into spring, experience the exhilaration of a long awaited summer, and keeping the priority of reading, writing and arithmetic at a high level is a daunting task. Though his teachers insist a summer reading program and mathematical practice is necessary if Will wants to keep up, the three month break and the call of the swimming pool have a way of making all of us conveniently forget the priority we once held so firm.

Even the most trying times don't guarantee a lasting shift in loyalty nor tragedy a steadfast, life-long commitment. Many have experienced terrible loss and in their pain and grief cried out to God, only to fall back into old habits and ways of living in a short period of time. We have witnessed this in the lives of individuals and even on a national scale. Terror strikes a nation and we turn to God. Death strikes a family and they look for answers to questions comfort has helped them avoid. Something shakes our normal routine so we shake-up our priorities. But when the dust settles how often do we go back to the ruts created over time in path of our lives? Is it possible to make our priorities stick? I think so. Here are a few thoughts we might want to consider.

PRIORITY CHANGE

Priorities can be altered rather quickly in the midst of tragedy or trials. Diets always have the best intentions until the holidays arrive. How do we stay committed to the right things and never go back? If we've learned anything from the Israelites it is that humans tend to regress. So let me suggest a few ways to keep our priorities in line.

1. *Make a list* — Make a list of your current priorities and your desired priorities. After you finish your list, ask someone

close to you to verify the truth of your present priorities and help you form a battle plan for change.

2. *Be intentional* — Begin to devote more of your resources to those things that are more important. Make specific commitments, don't just say I'll do better, what exactly will you do; what's the plan? At first this may be difficult and a sacrifice but eventually your emotions will catch up with your devotion.

3. *Ask For Help* — No one wants you to be unbalanced. Likely there are those in your life just waiting for the chance to help; if you would give them permission. The best way to get help is to ask. Ask your spouse, ask your kids, ask a friend, ask a pastor, but ask someone to help you change. Solomon wrote, "A chord of three strands is not quickly broken." (Ecclesiastes 4:13).

4. *Be Teachable* — Asking for help requires humility. But accepting and learning takes even more. Without humility we fail to listen, without it we fail to see, without it we fail to grow – without humility our new priorities haven't a chance. Sticking to our priorities requires a willingness to learn and be corrected, even by those younger or smaller or "less" important. Accountability is useless if we won't humble ourselves enough to be taught.

5. *Be Consistent* — Committing to a new set of priorities is a day by day process. Nevertheless it requires dogged, disciplined consistency. Nothing defeats our new life more than relapses. Nothing convinces our loved ones we're not really serious about change like inconsistency.

6. *Avoid Debt* — This may seem a little out of place here, until you examine the impact debt has on our priorities. Debt is a distraction from the journey. We can become so busy paying back for yesterday's thrills we have no time for today. When our finances are out of control our priorities slip. You may not be able to avoid debt completely, but the less you're controlled by it, the better you'll be able to dictate what receives your time.

7. *If at first you don't succeed … Keep trying—* If your priorities are really messed up this is going to take time and effort.
   Remember gradual change is better than no change. Attack
   priorities one at a time. Mixed-up priorities are bad habits
   that need breaking.
8. *Choose!—* Joshua looked at the people he had led into the
   Promised Land, his words, a challenge and a warning, rang
   through the vast throng, "CHOOSE!" (Joshua 24:15) After
   all is said and done priorities are a choice. They don't happen
   by accident. The best tools only benefit us if we are ready to
   make the right decisions. Choose your priorities carefully;
   they will dictate the rest of your life.

GIVING JESUS THE PRIORITY SLIP

The journey can only teach us priorities; not guarantee they'll
stay. The process may open our eyes to the need for change but we
must choose to remain changed.

Jesus experienced such fleeting loyalty in his day as well. Once,
on the way to Jerusalem, ten lepers cried out to him for mercy. Each
man faced the prospects of a continual life of pain and depression;
social outcasts, carriers of one of the worst diseases of the day.
Lepers didn't often desire to draw attention to themselves, but their
minds were made up, their priority was finding help, so they cried
out to Jesus.

Luke records that, "They called out to him in a load voice." Jesus
didn't go to them, they came seeking him. These were desperate
men. So what happened after Jesus met them? Once their need was
met how did they respond?

The story continues, "One of them, when he saw he was healed,
came back, praising God in a loud voice. He threw himself at Jesus'
feet and thanked him—and he was a Samaritan. Jesus asked, "Were
not all ten cleansed? Where are the other nine?"" (Luke 17:15-19).

Only one returned. Nine Lepers were too busy with their new
blessing, healing and life to give praise to the very one that made
it all possible. Maybe they were on a book tour, or participating in
some sort of traveling ministry. Maybe they were making up for lost

time, visiting relatives, or looking for work. We really don't know. All we know is that they weren't with Jesus.

Their God centered priority ended exactly after their need was gone. How often does God meet us when we call and our response is forgetful preoccupation? How often do we neglect even a simple, "Thank you"? No wonder some are never, *"made well."*

"When I say, 'I don't have time for this project,' I really mean, 'I don't consider it as important as something else I want or need to do." The issue is not simply a lack of time but a choice I make. The first step to regain control of time is to decide what activities are most important so that we can plan to give them the proper priority." Charles E Hummel from The Tyranny of the Urgent

Even the Israelites, with all they experienced, failed to train up the next generation. This account is given to us of their failure, "After that whole generation had been gathered to their fathers, another generation grew up, who knew neither the LORD nor what he had done for Israel. Then the Israelites did evil in the eyes of the LORD … They forsook the LORD..." (Judges 2:7,10-13).

All that their fathers learned from the journey the next generation lost in the destination. Even when we've arrived or accomplished something, we must remember there is still more traveling to do. The journey teaches us priority, but it is ours to keep.

The Pathway of Priority is meant to protect what really matters. Without the reality checks and eye-opening landscape of the journey we might never change. However, some priorities in our lives won't always be available to devote our time and energy to. Kids grow up and move away. Youth fades like the grass of the fields. Moments of divine inspiration disappear. And sometimes other priorities just get tired of waiting. Sadly, if we refuse to walk the pathway of priority some priorities may one day get up and walk away from us.

Yet above all else the supreme priority lies within the final discovery the Israelites made in their desert wandering. Put all other priorities to right, yet fail at this one and we fail everything. H.G.

Wells captured this truth when he wrote, "Until a man has found God, and been found by God, he begins at no beginning and works to no end."[19]

PONDERING PRIORITY:

1. You've read about it, now it's time to do it. Below is the Priority Check from the chapter. List what the following areas reveal about your top three priorities.

    - *Check book* _____
    - *Calendar* _____
    - *Consuming* _____
    - *Conversations* _____
    - *Convictions* _____
    - *Commitments* _____
    - *Character* _____
    - *Compassion* _____

2. What do your answers above reveal to you about your priorities?

3. As you evaluate your priorities what have you discovered are the main sources of distraction and time consumption? How will you reign in these enemies of God-centered priorities?

4. Look again at the Priority Change section of the chapter? Which of these will you incorporate to help in keeping your priorities straight? What other possible solutions might work for you?

Stop #5

"IS THE JOURNEY REALLY NECESSARY? – THE DESERT ROAD OF DIVINE DISCOVERY

Every conscientious parent has uttered these instructions to their little ones, "Don't talk to strangers!" And why not, there is sound reasoning to these protective words. Our world can be an unsafe place at times. And the unknown offers an uncertainty to security. So the request to be cautious is not an unreasonable command. In fact, most children grow up in the shadow of this common message.

Something drove my parents to warn me of the dangers of placing my trust in someone I didn't know. Yet I also grew up in a home that encouraged my belief in a God I could not see. *I'm supposed to stay away from strangers, but speak with an invisible God.* I didn't understand. It seemed more reasonable to trust someone I could hear, touch, and see then it was to trust a God I did not. I knew from the start, if I was ever to place my faith in the God of my parents I would have to know him personally.

Slavery really messed up the Israelites; especially when it came to following the God of their Fathers. Before the Exodus, they labored for a ruthless master in the shadow of false deities. Surrounded by these idols, their knowledge of "divine" things had been tainted. In addition, their relationship to the God of Abraham, Isaac, and Jacob

59

was limited and non-experiential. In short, they simple did not know their God. Not even his name.

The evidence of this is clear and consistent. Even Moses had to ask the Burning Bush the name of this God. To which God responded, "I AM WHO I AM. Thus you shall say to the sons of Israel, I AM has sent me to you'" (Exodus 3:14 NASB). A name of mystery, leaving more questions than answers.

The Hebrew form of "I Am WHO I AM," used in this verse indicates progressive action. By giving this name God was saying, "I know that you do not know me now, but I will demonstrate who I am by what I do."

But that wasn't enough for his people. In the process of revealing himself at Mount Sinai they turned to worshipping idols. When things became difficult the people cried out, "Why did we ever leave Egypt? Let us appoint a leader to take us back." (Numbers 14:3-4). Even bondage and slavery seemed more appealing than the unknown. They still did not trust Him.

So God took them through 40 years of wandering to humble their self-suffiency, to test their quality, to teach them priority, and to reveal Himself. In their journey God opened their eyes to the realities of who he was. This is critical. For if our knowledge of Him is off even just a bit, it will impact everything in our lives. Like a shirt that is buttoned even just one button too high or too low, so even a minor false view of God alters *everything* else.

> *"The world becomes a strange, mad, painful place, and life is a disappointing and unpleasant business, for those who do not know about God. Disregard the study of God, and you sentence yourself to stumble and blunder through life blindfolded, as it were, with no sense of direction and no understanding of what surrounds you. This way you can waste your life and lose your soul." — J.I. Packer from <u>Knowing God</u>*

The desert road was the way to divine discovery – revealing God's heart, proving His trustworthiness, and opening their eyes to witness His nature. God could have just told them who he was, but that wouldn't suffice. They must experience Him.

DISCOVERING GOD'S PRIORITY

Unlike men and women, God has no need to "get His priorities strait." He knows them well. He created that priority, He provides for that priority, and He even died for that priority. He reminded the Israelites of their standing, "Know then in your heart that as a man disciplines his son, so the LORD your God disciplines you. Observe the commands of the LORD your God, walking in his ways and revering him."(Deuteronomy 8:3; 5, and 6) God viewed his people through the eyes of a father. He only disciplined them to save them. *God's first priority is to rescue his creation.*

When the Israelites spied out Canaan the first time, they were filled with fear. The inhabitants of the land were powerful and intimidating. Yet above that, Israel did not trust God's love for them nor his ability to save.

Numbers records, "That night all the people of the community raised their voices and wept aloud. All the Israelites grumbled against Moses and Aaron, and the whole assembly said to them, "If only we had died in Egypt! Or in this desert! Why is the LORD bringing us to this land only to let us fall by the sword? Our wives and children will be taken as plunder." (Numbers 14:1-3).

They actually thought God was setting them up. They assumed he wanted to destroy them. How little they knew of this God; how foolish and blind their hearts to think the one who delivered them sought to do them harm.

> *"One way the enemy attempts to draw us away from trusting God is by perverting our perception of God's character." – John Bevere from his book <u>The Bait of Satan</u>*

In spite of their mistrust and constant complaining God never forsook His people. On the contrary, He faithfully led them; providing for their needs, revealing His character and proving that they were His chosen treasure.

God's top priority flows through the words of his Son, "I came to seek and to save that which was lost."(Luke 19:10). When words necessitated deeds God's son demonstrated God's priority; allowing himself to be nailed to a Roman cross. No accident, no scheme of man. The crucifixion was the ultimate statement of God's priority; a finely crafted, expertly executed, divinely directed revelation of God's unfailing love.

But God didn't stop there. *His second priority is to refine his creation.* God did not sacrifice his Son only to save us then watch us return to our past lives – back to Egypt. He redeemed us to refine us, to purify us and set us free. Not just from the penalty of death but from the daily prison of sin's grip. We've been rescued for a reason. That reason is to be refined. To be transformed into a new creation, one that much more resembles its Creator.

The Apostle Paul wrote, "Therefore be imitators of God" (Ephesians 5:1). But how does this happen? That's where God comes in. He began the work at the cross and brings it to completion throughout our journey (Philippians 1:6). It is God who refines. It is the clay that surrenders to his molding hands. Jesus said fruit would grow from branches that remained connected to Him (see John 15). So by his words we know that true transformation comes from an intimate connection to the Vine.

Writing this book was a process of creation. As I scribbled or typed the words and phrases that became a manuscript, countless revisions, additions, and subtractions filled the journey of making it complete. I did this, not because I found loads of free time at my disposal. Rather I revised, or refined, my creation so that after it was finished it would become the best work that I could possibly produce. And maybe, just possibly, as others read, they would see a noticeable reflection of its author hidden within.

Perhaps God is doing the very same thing in our lives. Others read, discovering what God has written into our story. "We are his workmanship" (Ephesians 2:10) and so God refines us; stroke by stroke, line by line, until we are exactly what he wants us to be; a creation reflecting the image of the Divine Author.

From Genesis to Revelation God's priority is clear. Many times he could have given up, left mankind to fend for itself, but he didn't. Even as the wind of self-will and rebellion blew across Eden and swept his creation away, God would not have it lost for long. From that moment forward he peered through the window of this world longing for the day he would buy his beloved back. Waiting for that hour, he slowly revealed his character to men, drawing them nearer.

Then with tears in his eyes and a final sigh, he lay down his son to purchase his defiant creation. "It is finished," the deal was made, the price paid. Priority is easily measured by how much one is willing to sacrifice. Wow, we sure mean a lot to God!

WITNESSING GOD'S PROVIDING POWER

Ten plagues unleashed upon Egypt. The waters of the Red Sea held back by the hand of God. The greatest military power of the day, annihilated before the eyes of slaves. This and so much more. But it wasn't enough to trust the I AM. Israel needed more proof. What allowed doubt to live in the face of such overwhelming evidence? Why weren't the big miracles enough? Because they didn't last.

Sure they witnessed God's fireworks but those don't instill trust, or promote intimacy. God's power awed them, struck fear into their hearts, and even made them grateful, but it did not endear Him to them. Instead of fireworks they needed his friendship. Faith grows best in the ground of consistency and intimacy.

The dessert road became the testing ground for their God; the place of relationship on the way. Within those moments they experienced his providing hand. 14,600 miraculous meals in the desert caused the people of Israel to trust and know him. He reminded them, "Your clothes did not wear out and your feet did not swell during these forty years. For the LORD your God is bringing you into a good land." (See Deuteronomy 8:4, 7-9, 15)

As with the Israelites we need to see the hand of God on a daily basis. It is then that we learn to trust him. We learn He is not just a God of the "Big event" but also of the "Basic everyday experiences." As we witness God's provision of our daily bread, we understand that He is more than a Christmas Jesus and an Easter Savior. The journey reveals to us that God can provide even the little things.

In the early years of our marriage, Tamara and I worked several jobs to survive. Along with coaching, working retail, and donating time to the church, I worked as a substitute custodian for a couple of public school districts in western Washington.

Late one night on my way home I noticed a car stranded on the side of the freeway. Its caution lights were activated and I could just make out the figure of a man resting on the passenger side door. I was in no mood to be helpful. Many problems lay heavy on my mind, particularly finances. The bills were due that week and I was still short $30.00 and some change.

With little enthusiasm, but a definite nudge of the Holy Spirit, I pulled just in front of the disabled vehicle to offer my assistance. The gentleman approached me with a smile and an extended hand. He thanked me for stopping and asked if I could drive him to the nearest gas station. No problem. I dropped him off at the Texaco service station and pulled away, eager to get home.

The next day I discovered an unfamiliar item in my car; a checkbook. Opening the top fold I saw a vaguely familiar face looking back at me, a driver's license. Of course! The face belonged to the man I helped just hours earlier.

I called the gentleman and set up a time to meet. A few hours later we arrived at the agreed upon location. He complimented my honesty and I presented him with his lost possession. Then just before I reentered my vehicle he reached out and shook my hand, leaving a small folded package in my palm. "Thanks again," he said and drove away.

Slowly I released my fingers, letting their contents spill into my lap. Tears began to fill my eyes. Unfolding the bundle of crumpled bills I counted the gift ... $31.00.

You will never know that God can provide unless you need Him to! Problems are fertile ground for miracles! God is strong, not just for a moment or in the miraculous, but in the ordinary, simple little things that show us we can trust him. In the journey we experience God's daily provision, producing faith strengthened with every deliverance. Louisa Stead penned the words to the familiar hymn,

"Jesus, Jesus how I trust you how I've proved you oe'r and oe'r. Jesus, Jesus precious Jesus, oh for grace to trust you more."[20]

"God cannot give us happiness and peace apart from Himself, because it is not there. There is no such thing."
- C.S. Lewis[21]

The Bible is full of stories of God's ability to provide and deliver. Shadrach, Meshack, and Abendigo boldly faced the flames because the I AM, waited in the fire. Elijah found himself surrounded, sharing a cabin with a terrified servant, yet it was the enemy hoard that came under siege. David was delivered from the hand of friend and foe; animals and giants. And a frightened young Queen Esther saved a nation in the face of certain death. Add your name and circumstance to the list. If it hasn't happened yet, it will. God will provide!

LEARNING GOD'S SOVEREIGNTY

There is an important final lesson learned by the people of Israel in the midst of their journey; a truth that many in the Christian church today have forgotten. God is in control. God is sovereign. He makes the rules, we do not. He chooses the answer to our prayers and no one else. He reminded Israel, "But remember the LORD your God, *for it is he* who gives you the ability to produce wealth." (Deuteronomy 8:18, emphasis mine).

Even when we do provide for ourselves or use our own abilities to accomplish something, God is still the source. King Solomon reminds us, "There is no wisdom, no insight, no plan that can succeed against the Lord." (Proverbs 21:30).

Witnessing God's power on our behalf can make us overconfident. Like the mouse that crossed the bridge with an elephant as his companion, we boast about our great accomplishments. With little regard for the help coming from above we say, "Boy, *we* sure rocked that bridge, didn't *we*?" To which God whispers back, "apart from me you can do NOTHING!" (John 15:5). Be certain of this, we may do some of the talking but God does all the rocking.

***"Sir, my concern is not whether God is on our side; my
great concern is to be on God's side, for God is always
right." – Abraham Lincoln*[22]**

We don't give God our plans so that he can move with us. We
find out what piece he wants us to play in his puzzle and then jump
in where he decides. A close friend and fellow pastor, often says,
"Don't ask God to join you, find out what he's doing and join Him."
The Word of God is clear; God is in charge.

*"Let them know that you, whose name is the LORD— that
you alone are the Most High over all the earth." — Psalms
83:18*

*"Our God is in heaven; he does whatever pleases him."
— Psalms 115:3*

*"Praise be to the name of God forever and ever; wisdom
and power are his. He changes times and seasons; he sets
up kings and deposes them. He gives wisdom to the wise and
knowledge to the discerning. He reveals deep **and hidden
things; he knows what lies in darkness, and light dwells
with him.**" — Daniel 2:20-22*

*"Who can speak and have it happen if the Lord has not
decreed it?"- Lamentations 3:37*

When Jesus faced Pilate, the Roman Governor attempted to use
his power to force him to cooperate. After all, Pilate reasoned, *I'm
the authority here.* He informed Jesus that his decision determined
Jesus' freedom or execution. At hearing this, Christ looked Pontius
Pilate square in the eyes and said, "You would have no power over
me unless it was given to you from above." (John 19:11). Jesus was
confident in the sovereign plan of God, he knew who was in control.
His fate would not be decided by any man.

Remember this next time your employer insinuates, "Don't you
realize I have the power to fire you?" Or your professor suggests,

"I could fail you," Or even the government declares, "We can fine you." No man has power above God. Jesus believed this fact and it caused him to trust and obey his Father, all the way to the cross and beyond.

But there's another side. When we think we call the shots with God it's not Biblical or healthy either. To hold and maintain the view that my God is so weak that I can control him is frightening. If I direct his paths and instruct him on the right course of action, who is really God anyway?

But I know who has the power and the wisdom and the knowledge to reign over my life, and I know my prayers don't manipulate or control Him. Instead of bothering me, these facts make me feel secure. I don't know about you, but I'd much rather have God in control than me. That is why, as I learn and accept that he is sovereign, I can continue my journey at peace, resting in all that *He is*.

GOD WHO?

How do you contain the uncontainable ... explain the unexplainable ... describe the indescribable? That is the task that awaits all who attempt to define God. Yet within his matchless nature key characteristics demand our attention. Continuing our journey without a biblical understanding of who God is could lead us down some pretty scary roads. So as we end our preparations for the journey let's take a look at a few important aspects of the nature of God.

God is Unchanging. The Bible teaches us that, "(God) does not change like shifting shadows" (James 1:17) and that, "He is the same yesterday, *today, and forever.*" (Hebrews 13:8) Why is this so important? If this were not true all of the other characteristics of God would be subject to mood swings, negotiations, and any number of variables that alter the character of Human beings. How could I count on his grace if it was unstable? How could I depend on his word if he changed his mind? How could we know anything for certain if God was not? But he is; He does not change. We rest securely in who he is because that is exactly who he always will be. "I the Lord do not change" (Malachi 3:6)

God is Love. There are many definitions of love. Perhaps no word is more misunderstood. We love our sports teams, we love pizza, we love a car — we use the word to get what we want or to show affection. We *fall in* and *fall out* of this kind of love and base it far too often on how we feel or how we are treated. But when the Bible says, "God is love," (1 John 4:8) it speaks of something much higher than any of these. Knowing that God is love we also know that he is patient, kind, unselfish, humble, meek, polite, giving, temperate, forgiving, good, truth, protecting, trusting, hopeful, and persevering. Because God is love we know He never fails. (See 1 Corinthians 13:4-8). And this is a love we can count on.

God is Holy. Jonathan Edwards once said, "A true love to God must begin with a delight in his holiness, and not with a delight in any other attribute; for no other attribute is truly lovely without this."[23] The absolute purity of God and weight of his majesty is the only characteristic repeated in scripture three time in succession, "Holy, Holy, Holy" (Revelation 4:8). In our knowledge of his love we must also understand the severity of his holiness; it demands justice. If not for the cross we would all stand hopeless and helpless, apart from God. We live now in the wonderful grace of his son, but this by no means erases his holiness. We would do well to remember, "Our God is a consuming fire." (Hebrews 12:29)

God is All-Knowing and Wise. "Nothing in all creation is hidden from God's sight. Everything is uncovered and laid bare before the eyes of him to whom we must give an account" (Hebrews 4:13). The fact that God knows everything is comforting – and disturbing. He knows the hearts and thoughts of men; he knows the future and the past. Nothing surprises him and nothing gets by him. Yet he is not merely all-knowing but all-wise as well. This provides confidence that in our lack of understanding we rest secure in the hands of a loving, holy, and wise God.

God is All-Powerful. "Ah, Sovereign Lord, you have made the heavens and the earth by your great power and outstretched arm. Nothing is too hard for you" (Jeremiah 32:17) God has no equal. He can't be defeated, he always wins, he has yet to even face a challenge and never will. When I know that God is loving, holy, and wise, I then rejoice in the fact the he is also unbeatable. The world and spiritual darkness rages around me yet I know God is far-greater than them all. "Yours, O Lord, is the kingdom; you are exalted as head over all" (1 Chronicles 29:11).

God is God Alone. "Before me no god was formed, nor will there be one after me. I, even I, am the Lord, and apart from me there is no savior ... I am God." (Isaiah 43:10-12) In a world of relativism and tolerance the truth has not changed. There is only one God. All other religious expressions, spiritual pursuits, deities and supernatural experiences are cleverly repackaged deceptions of an ancient lye. "There is no God besides me ... No one can deliver out of my hand!" (Deuteronomy 32:29).

THE JOURNEY BEGINS ...

The Apostle Paul prayed, "... that you may be filled with the knowledge of His will in all wisdom and spiritual understanding ... fruitful in every good work and increasing in the knowledge of God;" (NKJV Colossians 1:9-10).

The people of Israel learned who God was only as they traveled the dessert with Him. As they prepared to enter Canaan, God reminded them of their past to ensure a different future.

In our travels so far we've discovered at least three things. First the journey *is REALLY* necessary; we can't make it home without it. Second, to gain all we can from life we must pack accordingly. That means we travel with our medication; committed to slowing down, paying attention, and living focused on purpose. Finally, we've taken a good look inside of ourselves and found destination drivenness living within, causing us to miss many of the treasures life holds on the way.

These are important lessons, essential for any traveler who will be guided by the hand of God. Just as he did with Israel, our God leads us *through* many things to accomplish much *in* us. Sometimes the journey takes us to, "green pastures and beside still waters" and other times, "through the valley of the shadow of death ... and in the presence of enemies."(see Psalms 23). Each part has a purpose, each season a lesson.

God led Israel through the wilderness to humble them, to test their quality, and to teach them proper priority. He led them through the desert that they might know Him and discover all that he is. So, "Is the journey REALLY necessary?" ... If you want to make it to the Promised Land it is!

GOD THOUGHTS:

1. What are some misconceptions and wrong first impressions that people have about God? How might they impact how people live, act, and think?

2. How do people come to some of these half-truths and outright lies?

3. In what ways might your own view of God be off? How can we maintain a proper understanding of who God is?

4. Think about God's nature and activity in human history, are their thing about Him that comfort you? What are they? Are there things about Him that concern you? What might they be? Are their things about Him that confuses you? If you answered "yes" to any of these take some time with a spiritual mentor and the scriptures to dive deeper. Ask God to help you understand who he is and how to know him better.

5. How might a proper understanding of God coupled with an intimate relationship with Him change how you journey?

Stop #6

SIDE STREETS OF SETBACKS

The tears flowed freely, streaming down her wrinkled cheeks and dropping to the cobble stones below. She could not help them - anymore than she could cease their coming in the long days that preceded the finality of this occasion. Her loss haunted her every step. Its gravity deeply etched her face. So much loss in her life time, so much pain experienced. The questions echoed in her broken soul, "Why, Lord? Why, oh God? Why take my husband? Why strike my only child with a sickness? Why did my son have to die?"

There were whispers of a curse. Demonic affliction set against this woman's house. Others murmured that sin was behind such tragic suffering. The woman must be hiding dark secrets that remained unknown. Though God's punishment could be severe, it was always just.

They thought she could not hear – that she remained ignorant to the rumors. Yet their judgment showed on their faces and flashed in their eyes – even now in the center of her grief. These thoughts gave no reprieve, did nothing to sooth the sting. Pain clawed at her spirit like a wild animal tearing the very life from her being. A moan escaped her sun-baked lips. Her soul was broken – the shards scattered upon the ground.

The procession began its short trek outside the city gates. The cries and tears of professional mourners followed them to the grave. Though not far, the walk seemed an eternity.

What sin had she committed to deserve this? What faith had she lacked? The sin question made no sense. She was no worse than those around her, even better than some. Her faith was not so weak; she believed God and trusted him, most of the time. She could not understand how God could let this, or even worse, cause this to happen.

"Does God really care? If so, why won't he reach down and fix the things that go wrong – at least some of them?"
– Philip Yancey from, <u>Disappointment with God</u>

"Why? Oh God, why?" The questions reverberated through her mind bringing an ever increasing spring of tears. She felt anger, but more than that she felt … abandoned … forsaken ... alone … frightened … forgotten. Why did God turn so cruel? Why demand her only son? He took Isaac from Father Abraham. Yet Abraham was a man, he could take care of himself. Abraham received his son back, her sacrifice was final. Final as the grave. God allowed such pain, but He could never understand the loss of an only son.

Suddenly, the casket and its mourners stopped. This was not their destination, she knew these steps well. She'd walked them before following her husband's still body. Yet the procession paused as if ordered by a king to halt. She did not know why, and did not care. She had nothing left to live for, only tears.

Those around her began to mutter. A dusty man approached the childless widow. She stared at the ground unable to lift her head, the weight of the day too much to bear. Two sandaled feet appeared under her bowed head, her tears staining the worn leather straps. A gentle hand slowly lifted her shaking chin, cupping her face in calloused fingers. She looked into eyes that mirrored her pain, yet glistened with hope. Compassion and understanding shown from his face, a tender smile and a tear framing his words. Quietly he spoke, "Don't cry … God knows." (based upon Luke 7:11-15)

ANOTHER DAY – ANOTHER SORROW

"He's not coming! What do you mean he's not coming?" She could not believe her ears. After all they had done, after all the time spent with him, and now in their greatest need he wasn't coming? "Well, that's not quite what he said," replied the messenger.

"What did he say then? Please tell me," she pressed, "Did you tell him, 'Lord, the one you love is sick'?"

"I told him those words exactly." Pausing to remember the moment he continued, "He looked concerned, but he would not come. As I rode away I heard him say something to his disciples. I think he said 'this sickness will not end in death.' So he must be coming."

Martha thought for a moment and looked into her sisters questioning eyes. "When?" her younger sister asked, "When will the Lord come? I don't think our brother will last much longer."

Martha softly reassured her, "He will come … You heard the message. He will come, and he will come in time."

They both went to the window and peered down the road coming to Bethany - searching for the Lord, willing him to come now. Martha left her sister's side to tend to the needs of their brother. As she departed, Mary gently took hold of Martha's robe, tears falling from her eyes, she asked, "When?"

With an uncertain nod Martha caressed her sister's hand and mouthed the words, "I don't know, but he will come."

Mary went back to watching the road as Martha busied herself with chores. But the work couldn't push back the question.

Hours later, both women stood by their brother's side – his body stiff and lifeless. Lazarus was wrapped in cloths and prepared for burial. Men placed him in the tomb and covered the entrance. The thud of the stone sealed and doomed their hope. The "when" did not come in time.

"Never will I leave you; never will I forsake you." – God[24]

The Master was too late. The sickness had taken their brother, and their Lord was nowhere to be found. The one whom he loved had died and, either Jesus did not care, or he simply had better things to do. The "when" would come four days later – the sick bed empty, the tomb all too full.

For those four days Mary hardly left her place at the window. One word rolled through her mind, tormented her thoughts – "when."

As the Master approached she could not bring herself to go to him. What would she say? He had lied to them and failed them. Yet in her heart she still believed, wanted to trust, and loved him so much, no matter what.

Martha ran out of the house toward Jesus, her mind formulating the words she would speak. But as she ran she also remembered. Remembered his love, reflected on his miracles, reminded herself of who he was. Any anger, accusations, or questions quickly dissipated. One look into his eyes told her, he grieved too.

She looked into the confident tear stained face of the Master. "Lord, if you had been here my brother would not have died." Hoping she added, "… But I know that even now God will give you whatever you ask!"

Jesus looked into her face, with eyes of power and absolute certainty, and said, "Your brother will rise again … I am the resurrection and the life. He who believes in me will live, even though he dies … Do you believe this?"

A smile carved its way across her face, "Yes Lord, I believe in YOU!" Jesus matched her smile and made a simple request, "Go get Mary, I need to see her. She needs to see me."

Martha found Mary on her knees weeping, "When? When? When?" she cried! Martha raised her younger sister. With the faith acquired from the encounter with the Lord on the road, she spoke with conviction in the midst of her pain. "Mary, it doesn't matter anymore. HE is here!" (based on John 11:1-43)

LIFE CONQUERED - HOPE LOST

The stone was massive, larger than any of them expected. The Sabbath was over and so were their dreams.

Over the last two days all of life appeared to lose its wonder. The taste of food lost its pleasure. Drink did not satisfy. The joy of friendship fled away, just like the disciples that dreadful night in the garden. The followers of Jesus grieved behind closed doors, imprisoned in the walls of guilt and sadness.

But the grief seemed to affect more than those who knew him. Creation itself lost its splendor. The stars' brilliance faded. The moon darkened as the sun mourned in shadowed despondency. It was as if the entire universe felt the blows of the nails, the earth trembled as the spear punctured his side. The heart of the world went silent.

He was to be the solution to their problems, the long awaited reason for being, and the answer to all their doubts. But now he was gone. All that remained were problems, purposeless living, and questions.

This morning Mary Magdalene broke the weary silence with the first question, "Who will roll the stone away from the tomb?"

An obvious inquiry for the day's task, yet within it laid a deeper, more haunting question - one they dared not ask. For the stone had not merely sealed the dead body of their Lord, but their dreams as well.

The question Mary Magdalene really needed answered was, "How?" How could this tragedy be undone? No one had power to raise the dead, except Jesus. If he died, who would raise him up? Their friend and Lord was gone, their hope as dead as the body they removed from the cross. How could the life they expected be restored when *The Life*, lay dead, cold, and defeated by the grave? It was over, it was finished. Someone might roll the stone from the tomb, but their dreams were forever imprisoned behind death's cruel bars – decaying under Hell's merciless grip.

> *"And surely I am with you always, to the very end of the age." – Jesus*[25]

Then without warning, their thoughts and questions were violently interrupted. The ground began to shake, throwing them to the dirt path below. Mary, Jesus' mother, stooped to help the other women to their feet.

This day was proving to be difficult enough without an earthquake. But something shifted. Something within them suddenly felt

75

… alive again. The sky was bluer, the grass greener, the song of the birds in the garden seemed refreshed as well by new life. Coming to the tomb their question found an answer. For the sun itself perched upon the stone of the tomb, and the stone had been rolled away.

The brilliant light spoke to them; the angel's words and countenance reminding Mary of that day in Nazareth some 34 years ago. "Do not be afraid," he said, "I know you are looking for Jesus who was crucified. He is not here he is risen just as he said." Their question went unanswered, but they didn't need to know anymore. He was alive! (based on Mark 16:1-8 And Matthew 28:1-8)

THREE DEATHS, THREE QUESTIONS … ONE ANSWER

Death is as much a part of life as birth. In his book *Traveling Light*, Max Lucado observed, "We all have to face it. In a life marked by doctor appointments, dentist appointments, and school appointments, there is one appointment that none of us will miss, the appointment with death."

During the journey many things die. Dreams, hopes, health, comfort, reputations, marriages, and countless other possessions and passions get lost on the way.

Jesus experienced his share of death and disappointment. So did those he loved. They trusted God, but for some, when they needed him most, he wasn't there. In their pain he felt far away, distant, uncaring. The widow wondered "why" a loving God would take her son away. Mary questioned "when" would Jesus come into her desperate circumstances. The women at the tomb faced the most overwhelming setback of their lives and asked "how," could anyone overcome such an unmovable obstacle.

Some doubted themselves, others doubted him, but all had questions. Questions asked throughout history when life's journey overwhelms the weary traveler. When we are pushed beyond our preconceived limits, when the journey is beyond us, when we fail to understand or see the meaning behind the madness. When death's final nail is driven home we cry to the heavens, "Why? When? How?" The answers don't always come and rarely when we want.

Yet, in the Side Streets of Setbacks these questions are expected and natural.

- Mary asked the angel, "How can this be?" (Luke 1:34). An appropriate question for an unmarried virgin promised to give birth to the Messiah. Chosen by God for such a role was an honor, yet the ramifications would open Mary to shame, difficulty, and public scrutiny.
- Feeling alone and forsaken, asking when God would act on his behalf, David pleaded, "O Lord, how long (when) will you look on ... How long (when) O Lord? Will you hide yourself forever?" (Psalms 35:17 and 89:49).
- Even the Master asked "why" as he suffered at Golgotha. Jesus on the cross gasped, "My God, my God *why* have you forsaken me?" (Matthew 27:46) Yes, these questions are natural. But they're not adequate. Another question needs asking.

"When people are in difficulties, they want to cling to something. The only solution people here can believe in is Jesus Christ." — Rev. Johnson Makoti, a Zimbabwean minister[26]

The writer of Psalms 73, was frustrated by the health and wealth of the wicked. Asaph was irritated with God. His anger stemmed from the fact that while he struggled in his life, the unrighteous enjoyed great success. God did not give an explanation to Asaph's questions. Nonetheless, the Psalmist did find a solution. "When I tried to understand all this it was oppressive to me till *I entered the sanctuary of God;* then I understood their final destiny" (Psalms 73:16-17, emphasis mine).

The solution for Asaph was not the answers to his questions, but the presence of the Almighty. When he stepped out from his own quandary and into the realm of God, the only question he needed answered was, "Who?"

Even if God answered the "whys," would we understand? Even if the "whens" were in our timing, would it somehow make things better? Can we, with our finite minds and limited knowledge, grasp the "hows" when he works in his supernatural ways?

Set backs are not meant to present the solutions to our questions; they are there to abolish our need for them. They come to bring us to a much deeper place; to help us ask a much more important question – "*Who* is in control?"

The people who experienced the three deaths did not receive their answer. The widow asked, "*Why* did God allow this?" Mary and Martha asked, "*When* will he come?" The women traveling to the tomb asked, "*How* can anyone help?"

Their "setbacks" were final. Hope faded and life appeared bleak. But when the *Who* stepped into their pain, the questions lost their strength and power. When their eyes focused on the conqueror of the grave, death lost its sting and grief its victory.

Jesus stepped into the widow's pain soothing the "why" ...
because God knew her need.
Jesus stepped into Mary's loss erasing the "when" ...
because Jesus was there.
Jesus stepped out of the tomb astounding the "how" ...
Because He had risen!

When all of our questions and life's situations come face to face with the Risen Lord, the "Who" becomes enough. The pain, loss and grief still remain but we no longer face them alone.

"God may well be taken as a substitute for everything;
but nothing can be taken as a substitute for God."
– Anonymous[27]

FINDING THE ANSWER IN THE UNHAPPY ENDINGS

All travelers suffer. Setbacks come in various shapes and sizes. Some require a few weeks to recover from and others leave scars that never fade away. Some hurt for a moment, others haunt for a lifetime.

Maybe you have felt the chill of death's firm touch in your life. You ask, What about the funeral like the one you spoke of – the one that goes on uninterrupted? What of those who do not recover? What possible good could come from a premature birth, a child with leukemia, a chronic illness that condemns one to a life of pain? What great God glorifying gift could blossom from the terrible stench of a devastating accident, the destruction caused by natural disasters, a ruined marriage, or a violent rape?

Maybe your setback is less dramatic. Perhaps it is more inconvenient than life-threatening, more depressing than deadly. The death of a dream, the drudgery of doing a job you hate, a temporary yet dysfunctioning illness, or living in a place that drowns out your zest for life.

I must apologize. For your answers won't be found in this book. For that you need one much wiser than myself. In fact, you won't be satisfied with man's ideas when it is God's love and assurance you are looking for.

When you seek him He promises to meet you there. "Come near to God and he will come near to you" (James 5:8). "The Lord is close to the brokenhearted," the Psalmist wrote out of a depth of personal experience (Psalms 34:18). In a time of deep sorrow and national devastation Jeremiah was reassured by the Lord, "You will seek me and find me, when you seek me with all your heart" (Jeremiah 29:13). In his book *The Prayer of Jesus* Hank Hanegraff reminds us that our, "Brokenness is the road map by which we find our way back to an intimate relationship with God." And only at his side do we find what we need.

Job was a man who understood the Side Streets of Setbacks well. He asked questions that for a long period of time went unanswered by God, not to mention the eloquent false representations his friends had to offer. Job knew the hurt of loss and the sting of false accusations. He looked into the face of injustice and watched as his dreams were mercilessly torn to pieces by the onslaught of Satan himself.

"Where faith is easy, it is fading; where it's a challenge it thrives" – Nicholas Kristof, New York Times columnist[28]

Yet, Job was also a traveler who understood the bigger picture. In the midst of his confusion and calamities it was not the problems or questions that were important. Rather it was the One in the midst of everything that took precedence. So as he suffered, he also took courage in God, who was his source and salvation.

Job said, "I know that my Redeemer lives, and that in the end he will stand on the earth. And after my skin has been destroyed, yet in my flesh I will see God ... Though he slay me, yet will I hope in him ..." (Job 19:25 and 36 and 13:15)

Though Job suffered the loss of family, wealth, possessions, health, and even the respect of his wife and friends, he held on. When setbacks come, where do our eyes go? Job looked to God. When trials assault us, what do our hearts believe? Job believed God. When Satan attacks, what do our mouths speak? Job praised God. His mind was set upon *Who* his Redeemer was, not upon *what* his circumstances told him.

By the way, God did show up. And when He did, Job was vindicated and blessed with far more than he had ever lost. We have the same promise, if not in this life than in the next.

In the end, it's not what happens on this earth that matters most. The questions of "why, how, and when?" fail to supply what we really want to know. Our stronger need is to know, "Does God care? Who is in control? Can I trust him?"

"I had a thousand questions to ask God; but when I met Him they all fled and didn't seem to matter."
– Christopher Morley[29]

Life will present to each of us pain and suffering. It can't be avoided. What we need is what the widow found, what Mary saw, and *who* the women met at the tomb. Jesus knows your need, he is certainly with you, he is risen, and yes, he does care. And because he defeated death and the grave, so do we. Through the side streets of our journey — when we don't understand the pain — we can trust his goodness, we can trust his love …We can trust in *who* He is.

SEEKING GOD IN THE SETBACKS:

1. Have you ever experienced something that caused you to question God? Have you ever asked why did God allow this, when will God act, or how can this circumstance be over-come? What was the final result of your setback and search for answers?

2. What is the first thing you do when setbacks come? Is it more natural to trust in God or in someone or something else? Why?

3. On a scale of 1-10 how much do you really rely on God? How do trials impact this number?

4. What reassurance can you find in scripture about God's pres-ence in your setbacks?

5. What difficult situation might God use from your past to help others? What good things have or might yet grow out of the pain of your past?

THE BRIDGE OVER THE RIVER OF SUCCESS

A simple, nice father and daughter excursion was all that Allen had planned. He wanted to share a voyage with his eldest, to soak in the majestic beauty of the Montana wilderness. But the river had other plans.

The journey began as expected. They packed their gear, donned life preservers, and set out in the two man canoe. The watery solitude of the Missouri River presented Allen with the chance to spend time with his adolescent daughter – to share some advice and to talk about life. But the river had other plans.

The moment seemed perfect. Nature dazzled the adventurers with color and light. The scene was captivating, breathtaking, and mysterious as the water glistened in the fading sun. Then at the height of their revelry something happened. First a hard bump and then a sudden jerk, and the river had its way.

The canoe spun and capsized, throwing both passengers into the icy flow. An expedition meant to bring them together swept them farther apart. The rapids and current jostled them down stream. Rocks loomed as merciless predators. The chill and strength of the mighty river fought to take them to the bottom as they struggled to stay alive. Each breath a battle, each stroke a fight for survival.

Allen retells the story with vivid clarity, even years later. Both he and his daughter survived that unforgettable, perilous day. Yet they learned a valuable lesson. If not respected, beautiful rivers can prove dangerous – much like success.

Success is wonderful to admire as it shimmers in the light of adoration. It can be filled with fun and laughter. Take a drink and it can be quite refreshing. Step back and savor the many privileges fished from its pools, and it can bring satisfaction.

But launch out into its waters without caution, and its currents can quickly trap you; dragging you far from where you wanted to go, and who you wanted to be. Consume too much of its nectar, and success sours the stomach and bloats the soul. But there is a bridge over these troubled waters; a way to enjoy success without drowning in it.

"The purity of silver and gold is tested by putting them in the fire; the purity of human hearts is tested by giving them a little fame." – Proverbs 27:21 (MSG)

JOSHUA'S GREATEST FALL WAS NOT JERICHO'S WALL

Success can be a blessing or a curse; it just depends on how you handle it. Many in scripture found success, yet few of them noticed the bridge spanning its depths.

Take Joshua. As Moses' faithful apprentice, he studied everything this wise leader said and did. He stuck close to Moses' side, learning all he could.

When Moses went to the mountain of God, he traveled "with Joshua his aide" (Exodus 24:13). When the people sinned against the Lord in the shadow of Mount Sinai, Joshua held his place at Moses side – waiting on the Man of God as the man waited on His Lord (Exodus 32:17-18).

Joshua was faithful in his service to Moses and humble enough to stand in his shadow. He demonstrated a heart after God, rivaling that of even his mentor. "The LORD would speak to Moses face to face, as a man speaks with his friend. Then Moses would return to the camp, but his young aide *Joshua son of Nun did not leave the tent*" (Exodus 33:11 emphasis mine). Joshua stayed behind. He couldn't bear to leave. *Just a little more of God's presence*, he must have thought.

But soon after Joshua took the reins from Moses the mighty waters of success began to flow. A man full of potential would soon face the full potential of victories' ability to back fire when over-confidence goes unchecked.

In his first major battle Joshua took on the mighty city of Jericho. After crossing the Jordan River and celebrating the Passover in the plains surrounding the city, Joshua received a special guest. "Now when Joshua was near Jericho, he looked up and saw a man standing in front of him with a drawn sword in his hand" (Joshua 5:13). This man was none other than the "commander of the army of the LORD." Joshua asked for a plan, and God answered.

So the people of Israel walked a few miles every day, endured a little ridicule, and on the seventh day held a million-man rock concert that, literally, brought down the house. In one miraculous foot-stomping shout the entire city fell.

The cheers rang out, "Joshua, you're the MAN!" The victory was utterly complete, no contest. The coaching legend had been replaced and his protégé claimed the trophy. Of course, God did the wall smashing, but the success was undeniable. And this is where the trouble began.

Following the victory, Israel prepared to attack Ai — A small two letter town hardly worth noticing – a handful of warriors against the mighty Jericho-thumping armies of Joshua. And that may be exactly what they thought … until they were routed and sent running home to mamma.

Why such a defeat? That's what Joshua wanted to know. Was it simply because Achan stole some of the "devoted things"? Did just one man cause this humiliation? The answer is yes, but the guilt lay with Joshua.

Now wait a minute, Joshua was the leader. Exactly. Often when God's people fall, leadership stands as one of the culprits. And Joshua's critical mistakes, not Achan's greed, were the reasons for defeat.

Joshua's first miscue was forgetting to pray – his most critical mistake. In this second battle plan, Joshua did not hear from God (see Joshua 7:2-4). At Jericho Israel won because their leader listened to the directives of the Lord and followed through. Absolute obedience brought absolute victory. Yet before the skirmish against Ai no such meeting occurred. By his prayerlessness Joshua told God, "Don't worry about Ai, we've got this one handled." Failure was reaped because prayers went unsown.

The next error rested where Joshua placed his trust. His advisors against Ai were the spies sent to scope out the situation. Not God. Joshua listened too much to the people and too little to the Lord.

Leaders are only able to listen to so many voices and Joshua chose to listen to others and not to God. If he sought God before the battle, would God not have revealed the sin? Certainly God would have told Joshua. For when Joshua prayed in his humiliation, God answered, "Stand up! What are you doing down on your face? Israel has sinned" (Joshua 7:10-11).

Thirty-six fighting men lay dead upon the ground outside Ai, their blood stained the earth they sought to trample and celebrate over. Thirty-six daddies would not come home because God's chosen shepherd chose to follow man's opinion rather than seek God's.

The final mistake made the first two possible. How could a man who once humbly sought God fail to follow that pattern later? The answer is simple – success. The greatest fall in the life of Joshua arrived soon after the destruction of the walls of Jericho, not with them. Joshua leaned upon his past success to pull him through. That's when everything went terribly wrong. The river of success swallowed another victim, thirty-six to be precise.

A WISE HEAD BLOATED BY SUCCESS

Like Joshua, Solomon met with unparalleled success. The Bible tells us that, "King Solomon was greater in riches and wisdom than all the other kings of the earth." (2 Chronicles 9:22) Blessed with God-given wisdom, his fame spread throughout the world as his wealth and power exceeded his wildest imagination.

Many came to inquire of the King. Admirers ranged from prostitutes to queens and everyone in between. They all clamored for even a brief moment of Solomon's attention. "The whole world sought audience with Solomon to hear the wisdom God had put in his heart" (2 Chronicles 9: 24). Truly, King Solomon was successful. But as his fame gained strength his love for God began to lose ground.

Solomon's hunger for pleasure soon overwhelmed his wisdom. "King Solomon, however, loved many foreign women ... the LORD had told the Israelites, 'You must not intermarry with them, because they will surely turn your hearts after their gods.' Nevertheless, Solomon held fast to them in love" (1 Kings 11:1-2).

"Ability will enable a man to get to the top, but it takes character to keep him there." E.C. McKenzie[30]

Intoxicated by their beauty and the waters of success, Solomon plunged deep into the swift flow of the river of self and pride. His success polluted his priorities. A thousand wives and concubines filled his heart as the God who gave him everything was squeezed out.

HOW TO HANDLE SUCCESS – FINDING THE BRIDGE

Joshua and Solomon began their journeys with great promise. Ai was a hard lesson, but Joshua learned from it. The next time he avoided the water and took the bridge instead. Success can be a dangerous intoxicant, because it makes us delusional, exaggerating our own capabilities. For Joshua, the error was a hiccup in a life devoted to God. Not so for Solomon.

Solomon never did recognize the danger of his success. In his latter years, Solomon succumbed to his wives' false religions - finishing his journey a shell of the man he once was. The scriptures show just how far down stream he drifted, "As Solomon grew old, his wives turned his heart after other gods ... (He) was not fully devoted to the LORD his God ... Solomon did evil in the eyes of the LORD." (1 Kings 11:4-6)

While some travelers fall in the Side Streets of Setbacks, many more stumble in these avenues of achievement. But its dangerous rapids don't have to be deadly. Many fine men and women of God have come before us, crossing these waters with their integrity intact.

How might we learn to enjoy our successes without allowing them to swallow us whole? Let me direct your gaze toward the bridge that spans the river. On its wood planks are written six principles for making it across safely, securely and without getting soaked.

SAVOR SUCCESS AS A BLESSING FROM GOD

A damp, stormy February night set the stage for one of the greatest achievements of my life. In 1991, I earned a spot in the Washington State High School Wrestling Championships.

In the confines of the expansive Tacoma Dome, 4000 spectators looked down from the stands above. My father sat at the edge of the mat flanked by my head coach. My opponent warmed up on the adjacent side. I knew him well. Last year we met in this same location, and I lost. The feelings of failure pushed me to train harder and work longer than ever before.

Now only six minutes and my rival separated me from winning a state championship. I circled my side of the mat; then knelt to pray. I stripped off the warm-up shirt that read, "Glorify God through athletics," and placed it in my father's hands. The whistle blew. The match began.

To spare you the gory sweaty details, I'll just skip to the end. As the final seconds ticked away I looked back into the tearful eyes of my father. It was over. Nothing could change the result. I shook my opponent's hand as we congratulated each other on successful seasons and a competitive match. Then I turned, looking into my father's face. With all the emotions of the moment I flew into my Dad's arms. But unlike last year it wasn't for consolation. This year … I won.

I tell you this story because – well, it's really fun to remember, especially 18 years and 90 pounds later. But also to illustrate that success need not be a curse if handled correctly. For my Dad and I, nothing will ever replace that moment. Since that time we've spoken of it often and even watched the videos. That success has become a bridge to places where "preachers" are not always welcome.

James, the brother of Jesus, wrote, "Every good and perfect gift is from above, coming down from the Father of the heavenly light" (James 1:17). I believe that God wants to give us success. Too many times we fall into a trap of doubting our successes and exaggerating our failures. We don't enjoy it when something succeeds or belittle it as just "lucky."

This is not humility nor is it gratitude. Success is a gift not to be ignored but appreciated. By trivializing our accomplishments we damage the confidence needed to try new opportunities, the faith to pursue new adventures. Humility is found in savoring the blessings of God not ignoring them. These successes are gifts to be prized - our Heavenly Father wants us to enjoy them.

When I give my son a gift I delight in the pleasure it gives him. The joy in his voice, the gleeful giggle, the excitement and the big bear hug – each of these are priceless. And they make me want to give him more.

I believe God receives praise when we enjoy and appreciate the successes he allows into our lives. The Father heart of God loves to hear us laugh. He is with us through our tears, but how he cherishes our moments of childlike glee - when our hearts are filled with joy from his gracious blessing. So savor every success. It comes from the God who loves to see you smile.

GIVE GOD HIS DUE

As you savor success, remember the source of those blessings. To rightly handle success we must give "honor to whom honor is due" (Romans 13:7).

Maybe you've seen them – the victorious athlete giving honor to Jesus Christ for his triumph, the musician crediting God for his talent, the business man applauding the Lord for his wealth. It always makes me feel good to see this. Why? Because the One who deserves the glory is getting what he deserves.

And what he deserves is more than words. We can say, "I give glory to God." Yet still act in ways that displease him. Giving God the credit for our success is more than lip service. It means walking, in the midst of our accomplishments, with an attitude and in actions that show he's really in charge of our lives.

His blessings should lead us to bless others. His generosity should motivate us to live holy lives. The man, who gives God glory but hoards his millions, or points to the heavens but walks in pride and impurity, is missing the point.

All talent is God-given. To avoid the swift waters of success, that's exactly where the glory for those talents belongs. We can exalt ourselves or God, we can't do both. At a local basketball game I witnessed a young man who understood this principle. David is a solid Christian whose faith has weathered some tough times. Yet in the face of pressure he has stood strong.

Basketball is a game of give and take, and one of those gifts handed out are fouls. The night I sat at David's game, an opposing player bestowed such a gift on my friend. David strode to the line to shoot two free throws. As he dribbled the ball, something quite unexpected occurred. The entire student body of this public high school lifted their hands high in the air and with two fingers formed the sign of a cross. When the ball dropped through the hoop the students shouted "Amen."

David had touched an entire school with his faith in Christ. I looked on in admiration, proud of this young man whose success had not gone to his head, but to his God.

Like neon signs pointing to a restaurant's door, we have a purpose; but we are not the purpose. The sign isn't the reason; it is up there for *another's* promotion. It hangs and illuminates so that those who are searching will know what's inside. But they'll only know Him, if we give God his due.

"In the same way, let your light shine before men, that they may see your good deeds and praise your Father in heaven." - Matthew 5:16

DON'T TRUST SUCCESS

Success can be addictive. Let's face it. Presented with the choice to succeed or fail, which would you choose? Most prefer to be the victor not the victim. I know I do.

Success is fun, but if we're not careful we can become dependent upon it – to trust in our accomplishments and achievements, our wealth and popularity. The Apostle Paul warned, "Command those who are rich in this present world not to be arrogant nor to put their hope in wealth, which is so uncertain, but to put their hope in God" (1 Timothy 6:17).

Solomon's trust in fame sealed his fate. "His *fame* spread as far as the border of Egypt, because he had become very powerful … His *fame* spread far and wide" (2 Chronicles 26:8 &15 emphasis mine). Joshua met with the same notoriety after Jericho, "So the LORD was with Joshua, and his *fame* spread throughout the land" (Joshua 6:27). Both men won fame and power, but what damaged their lives was placing their trust in it.

Jesus also experienced the rise of fame and success. But he understood their fleeting and fickle nature – Jesus knew their uncertainty. One moment the crowds stood in amazement, and the next tried to throw him off a cliff (see Luke 4:20-30). John tells us, "But Jesus would not entrust himself to them, for he knew all men … he knew what was in a man." (John 2:24-25)

Jesus entered Jerusalem to shouts of praise, "Hosanna to the Son of David!" "Blessed is he who comes in the name of the Lord!" then days later heard those same voices growl, "Crucify! Crucify!" (Matthew 21:9 and 27:12-13). The disciples who vowed to die with him, only hours before, couldn't even find the courage to stand with him. Jesus knew success as a raging river, not to be trusted. It can turn quickly and in unexpected directions.

There's nothing wrong with success as long as we don't bet our lives on it, nor become intoxicated by its pleasing aroma. Jesus is where we place our trust because, unlike the waters of success, he is the, "same yesterday, today, and forever" (Hebrews 13:8)

"Like perfume, success is to be sniffed, not taken internally." – Russ Reid[31]

KEEP QUIET

I love Peter – his tongue was a double-edged sword. One moment he would converse upon the most divine revelations, then turn around and speak like the devil himself. You may think I'm being a little rough on Peter, so judge for yourself.

On the way to Caesarea Philippi, Jesus asked his disciples, "Who do people say I am?" They replied, "Some say John the Baptist; others say Elijah; and still others, one of the prophets." "But what about you?" he asked. "Who do you say I am?" Peter answered, "You are the Christ.'" (Mark 8:27-29)

All right Peter! Jesus asks a question, the rest of the disciples run around it, but not Peter. He lifts up his hand and boldly announces to the rest of the class the correct answer. He reveals his sensitivity to God and his faith in Jesus. What an awesome moment! All of a sudden Peter is looking pretty good. Maybe he even thought to himself, "Ha ... take that John and James, the places next to Jesus in his Kingdom have been filled."

Proverbs says, "A man finds joy in giving an apt reply – and how good is a timely word" (Proverbs 15:23) and, "Gold there is and rubies in abundance but lips that speak knowledge are a rare jewel" (Proverbs 20:15). Peter found himself in a "feel good" moment of success in ministry. Too bad he didn't have the added wisdom to keep his mouth shut.

Not long after his triumphant proclamation, Peter speaks again. Only this time Peter's mouth leads him astray – face first into the mud.

Jesus informed his disciples he would soon face suffering, rejection, and death, and that in three days he would rise again. Peter *rebukes* Jesus, correcting the Son of God. The same one who complimented Peter's faith earlier, now presents him with a new name, "Get behind me, Satan! You do not have in mind the things of God, but the things of men" (Mark 8:31-33).

Splat! Peter went from the rank of prophet to the reek of the pigpen. His declaration of faith and the subsequent success, made him arrogant – so much so he thought himself wise and lofty enough to rebuke God. Wisdom tells us, "When words are many, sin is not absent, but he who holds his tongue is wise" (Proverbs 10:19). Too bad Peter forgot this proverb. Too bad we do too.

Often success is best handled with silence. Yet accomplishments prove difficult to contain. We want to raise our hands in triumph and pump our fists victoriously in the air. After all, others need to know how good we really are. But all of this shouting makes us the main attraction, not God (not to mention a pretty big target for the Enemy).

Next time we find ourselves blessed with success, let us remember to ask God for a little self control and restraint as well. These two disciplines will help keep our feet on the ground, and out of our mouths. With success, silence is more than golden. It may be the best solution.

"Let another praise you, and not your own mouth; someone else and not your own lips." – Proverbs 27:2

GUARD WHAT MATTERS MOST

Albert Einstein once said, "Try not to become a man of success, but rather try to become a man of value."[32] Value is gained not through accomplishments, but by guarding what matters most. Success must never become the most important measurement.

Some say, "winning isn't everything," but I tend to disagree. In fact, winning is everything, many are just trying to win at the wrong game. When observing what our culture values most, who can blame them?

We worship those who are skilled at using a ball or a stick to score points and make money. Change the games and modify the instruments, but that pretty much sums up what many in our culture applaud. We celebrate those who sing, dance, act, or who are attractive or charismatic. So skill, ability, talent, looks, and money become the trinkets we run after. To handle success properly is to redefine its true identity.

Paul wrote to the young man named Timothy, "For physical training is of some value, but godliness has value for all things, holding promise for both the present life and the life to come" (1 Timothy 4:8). Proverbs 31 describes the source of real beauty, "Charm is deceptive, and beauty is fleeting; but a woman who fears the LORD is to be praised" (Proverbs 31:30).

"We who sit in history's bleachers are inclined to confuse fame with greatness. We seem to be willing to let the press, television, and radio determine whom we shall call great. Prominence, however, is a poor yardstick with which to measure greatness." Author Unknown[33]

True greatness is measured by how diligently we protect that which is important; those things that cannot be bought or sold. Our character, our families, our faith, and our destiny must not be neglected or traded for the fleeting trophies our culture worships. These idols do not provide life and are unworthy of our devotion.

When experiencing successes of a temporal nature, we must see them for what they are: *Temporary* blessings, and nothing more. By doing this we can protect those things which are much more important — the trophies that go with us after this life — those that reap rewards on the other side.

Perhaps winning *is* everything, especially when our focus is the prizes God offers. Don't spend all your time winning the games that don't last, rather "Run in such a way as to get *the prize*" (1 Corinthians 9:24). When success comes, guard your priorities, guard your soul, guard your character and, "above all else, guard your heart, for it is the wellspring of life" (Proverbs 4:23).

"Being first to cross the finish line makes you a winner in only one phase of life. It's what you do after you cross the line that counts" — Ralph Boston, Olympic Gold Medallist[34]

SUCCESS IS BEST SHARED NOT STORED

Though not an avid fan, from time to time, I will spare a few minutes to watch the various entertainment award shows. Whether the Oscars, Golden Globes, People's Choice, Emmy, or Grammy awards, it intrigues me to witness high paid entertainers verbally stumble all over themselves. What a sight.

Talented, beautiful, professional, people awkwardly bumble and blunder like second graders presenting their first speech to the class. Through clumsy, drawn out speeches they attempt to thank everyone who had anything to do with their award.

In their gracious generosity, these celebrities utilize an important tool to keep success in perspective. They remind themselves, "I could not have done this alone." And neither can we.

Every single great deed relies on a number of great contributors. The Apostle Paul wrote, "The body is a unit, though it is made up of many parts; and though all its parts are many, they form one body. So it is with Christ" (1 Corinthians 12:12). Success is never the work of one individual, rather an entire network or "Body" of people properly working together.

Happy endings begin with many unsung heroes. When you succeed, honor those who took part – don't just take the glory for yourself and store it away – share it. Make someone else look good, encourage others, honor their part in it, no matter how small. The river of success is much easier to master when you're not alone.

"The purpose in life is not to win. The purpose in life is to share. When you come to look back on all that you have done in life, you will get more satisfaction in the pleasure you have brought into other people's lives than you

will from the times that you outdid and defeated them."
— *Rabbi Harold Kushner*[35]

A SUCCESSOR WHO HANDLED SUCCESS "WISELY"

As a teenage boy, King David tasted the cool waters of success. The prophet Samuel visited his Father's house, meeting his older brothers, yet it was this dirty shepherd boy who caught God's attention. Samuel anointed David as the next king of Israel – the river of success began to flow.

Soon after, King Saul requested David's service. His unique gifts of music and poetry brought him face to face with the man he was anointed to replace. David used his skills to serve his king, not bragging of his experience with Samuel.

Then the day arrived and the river rose. A sling, a stone, and a giant's fall – broke open the flood gates. The river of success lay before him – how would he respond?

Overnight David became a household sensation. In a matter of seconds he transformed from lowly sheep-herder to national hero. As women shopped in grocery stores, the chatter and gossip spread. Teenage girls desperately searched to find "David the Giant Killer" posters.

Young boys traded playing cops and robbers for "shepherd boys and uncircumcised giants." Action figures and t-shirts, work out videos, and "how to" books raced off the shelves as, "all Israel and Judah loved David" (NKJV 1 Samuel 18:16).

Around the water coolers, in cafeterias, and over coffee cup conversations, everyone everywhere spoke of David. When it seemed he reached the peak of greatness, David proved them wrong, setting a new standard for what it meant to be a soldier in Saul's army. Even breaking the records held by the king. "Saul has slain his thousands and David his ten thousands" (NKJ 1 Samuel 18:7).

Given so much love and fame how would David respond to his popularity? With the smell of anointing oil still fresh in his memory, how would David act? "And David behaved *wisely* in all his ways, and the Lord was with him. Therefore, when Saul saw that he behaved *very wisely*, he was afraid of him" (NKJ 1 Samuel 18:14-15 emphasis mine).

With the increasing fear, jealousy and anger of the King would David change his tune? No, "David behaved *more wisely* than all the servants of Saul, so that his name became *highly esteemed.*" (NKJ 1 Samuel 18:30 emphasis mine) Though highly esteemed and incredibly successful, David viewed his accomplishments with the appropriate self-image. He was a soldier serving his nation and a man serving his God.

The word "wisely" comes from the Hebrew word "sakal."
This word literally means to be or act circumspectly,
vigilant, watchful. David experienced true success only
through wise and watchful action. In other words, success
is only success if handled correctly.[36]

Now, David had his moments. Later in life he let success go to his head. But the wise foundation built early in life always brought him back to where he belonged. So he met the river of success head on and chose to cross the bridge. He remembered it was God who got him there and God who would lead him safely to the other side.

Success can be a trap ... if you let it. But handled correctly it can be a beautiful blessing for all to enjoy. God intended you to have "life more abundantly" (see John 10:10). So take the gifts and blessings He rains down, and enjoy them. And when you face your own river, remember Solomon, known for his wisdom yet recognized for his fall. Then choose to travel like David, and behave like the shepherd boy — behave wisely.

CHOOSE WISELY:

1. How can we savor success as a gift from God? How can we make sure God knows how much we appreciate his gifts and, even more, the Giver?

2. When success comes how can we make sure God receives the credit? How should we live so that we don't bring discredit to his name?

3. Have you ever relied on past success and have it backfire? How can we enjoy success without leaning on it?

4. How will not "blowing your own horn" help you maintain balance with success? What character traits will be molded in your life by following this principle?

5. How do we guard our hearts from focusing on the wrong things? How do we make sure we are winning the right game?

6. Think about past successes. Have you shared the credit? Is it difficult when others get the credit, even if you should have? What might God be molding in your life through this? In what ways might we live to make others succeed?

Stop #8

THE BACK ALLEYS OF TEMPTATION

Dark alleys bring us face to face with childhood fears. The light is shrouded, the night cold and uninviting. Maybe your alley of fear took the form of a country corn field or a thick sage forest. Or perhaps an abandoned warehouse or foggy waterfront.

Whatever the place and particulars, most have experienced the sensation of feeling alone, but not certain you are. Adrenaline rushes through our veins as our imaginations take complete control of our sensibilities, stirring remorse for the time we snuck into that scary movie back in sixth grade.

I remember one such moment in my life. It was a chilly October morning in my freshmen year of high school. Determined to make the varsity wrestling team, I woke before dawn to begin my training.

In "Rocky-esque" fashion I adorned my body with several layers of ragged sweat clothes and headed out. The first leg of my journey passed through a well lit neighborhood with houses on either side, making it relatively pleasant despite the hour. However, the return trip home and the alternate path I chose; proved far less pleasurable.

Like the traveler who chooses the short cut, with menacing trees and dark shadows disclosing possible danger ahead, unease began to shroud my mind. The farther I went, the darker it grew. Looming trees replaced illuminating light posts, smooth sidewalks trans-formed into slick broken pavement.

Noises came from the underbrush and lingered from shadows behind. But wait, what did I have to fear? I was a championship caliber wrestler, I was in high school, I was in shape … I was terri-fied. As my anxiety increased so did my speed. I huffed and puffed and ran home as fast as my legs could carry me.

Well, I lived to tell the story, and from that day forward, found it more beneficial to train after school, in full daylight.

In the midst of that darkness only a few options were available to me; run, fight, or give up. When it comes to the Back Alley of Temptation our choices are not much different. You may say the wise traveler avoids such situations, and you would be right. But when it comes to this Back Alley, avoidance is not possible. Temptation is a place we all must face. Abraham, Joseph, Samson, King David, Judas Iscariot, Simon Peter, even Jesus Christ himself all forged through this alley.

It really is not a question of *if* you will go through this dark and ugly place; it is a matter of *when*. When the grim walls close in, your response determines your destiny. Proverbs Chapter Seven provides a detailed road map. And though the main character proved to be a miserable failure in his journey, his folly reveals our salva-tion through the Back Alley of Temptation.

RECOGNIZING THE ENEMY

The story begins with two primary characters; a foolish young man and a wily seductress. The woman is looking for a victim, the boy, a "good time." He starts down her street, looking both ways for eyes that might report his indiscretion. Like the internet surfer peeking at pornography or the business man abusing his expense account, at the right moment he ducks into the alley, hoping his choice goes unnoticed.

There she is, in all her beauty and allurement. She makes offers, provides promises and showers him with deceitful compliments, assuring him the pleasure will be immeasurable and the possibility of being found out remote. She looks good, sounds good, and has prepared everything. But in truth she is a spider calling her prey into a deep dark web from which his purity and potential will never return.

We've all heard her voice; we know the path to her door. And lust is only one of her enticements. Gossip, criticism, jealousy, pride, anger and greed are some of her more popular traps. In one form or another we've all entered into her net and paid the price for our choices.

The Bible exposes this truth, "There is no one righteous, no not one … For all have sinned and come short of the glory of God," (Romans 3:10 and 6:23). Yes, we have all failed, but we need not fail again. There are common characteristics found in every Back Alley of Temptation. Knowing them gives us the upper hand, providing a plan for victory.

> *"But each one is tempted when, by his own evil desire, he is dragged away and enticed. Then, after desire has conceived, it gives birth to sin; and sin, when it is full-grown, gives birth to death." – James the brother of Jesus*[37]

THE FACE OF TEMPTATION

To defeat temptation we must first recognize it. Many times we fall into temptation because we don't see the danger. We see the pleasure, the mystery, the escape, the promise of fulfillment; but not the monster in disguise. Sin has a way of deceiving us, making us believe *it*, rather than *God,* will fill the void in our lives. But we need not buy this lie, we can unmask our enemy.

Don't be deceived; sin doesn't just sit back waiting for someone to destroy. Temptation is an ***aggressive*** enemy. Look at how this seductress presents herself to our naïve young man. "Then *out came* a woman to meet him, dressed like a prostitute with *crafty intent* … *She took hold of him* and kissed him." (Proverbs 7:10, 13 emphasis mine)

She didn't wait for an invitation she attacked. The Bible warns of the aggressive nature of "her" seduction. "Be self-controlled and alert. Your enemy the devil prowls around like a roaring lion looking for someone to devour." (1 Peter 5:8).

Joseph met her on the way to the Palace. She dressed in the guise of Potiphar's wife, but it was still her. Joseph was still a slave, but for temptation it's never too soon to steal potential. Joseph tried to do his best with a bad situation, but in the midst of good intentions he still became the desired prey of a hungry predator. This lioness however, did not crave his life but his company, his intimate company.

Potiphar's wife hounds him, hunts him, and uses every trap, trick, and tactic at her disposal. She wouldn't take no for an answer. And when "no" became the only answer she would receive, she tried to have him killed – for a crime he didn't commit. The very one she tempted him to perpetrate.

How many times have the words been uttered, *"But I didn't intend to!"* The truth is many do not, but our enemy is aggressive. Our passivity or ignorance only leads to failure.

The aggressive nature of temptation is only half the picture. If it were merely aggressive, the battle would rage on the outside, pitting us against an enemy we despised. But temptation's strongest weapon is its attraction. "I have covered my bed with *colored linens* from Egypt. I have *perfumed* my bed with myrrh, aloes, and cinnamon. Come, let us *drink deep of love* till morning ..." (Proverbs 7:16-18 emphasis mine).

What if she would have approached him in a ratty bath robe, morning breath, and tooth decay? What if her bed smelled of old Limburger cheese, rotten onions, and was filled with moldy bread crumbs? How effective would she have been then? But temptation always presents itself in the best light. Temptation is **attractive**.

Even the Bible acknowledges there are "pleasures of sin for a season" (Hebrews 11:25). Let's admit it. Temptation would not be so hard to fight if it wasn't so ... well, tempting. If it didn't look so good, this fight would be relatively easy. The fact that there is a part of me that wants what it offers, makes temptation the greatest enemy I will ever face.

Remember Eve in the garden, "When the woman saw that the fruit of the tree was *good* for food and *pleasing* to the eye, and also *desirable* for gaining wisdom, she took some and ate it." (Genesis 3:6 emphasis mine) If Satan offered a clump of dirt or a pile of weeds, how might her response been different? But the serpent was too crafty for that; he offered Eve what she wanted, and she took it. The attractiveness of temptation takes the battle to another level, making it an intimidating inner struggle.

> *"So I find this law at work: When I want to do good, evil is right there with me. For in my inner being I delight in God's law; but I see another law at work in the members of my body, waging war against the law of my mind and making me a prisoner of the law of sin at work within my members. What a wretched man I am! Who will rescue me from this body of death?" – The Apostle Paul[38]*

The best way to fight the attractive nature of temptation is to focus on something possessing greater attraction. Perhaps for this very reason, scripture exhorts us to fix our eyes on Jesus (Hebrews 12:2). Temptation is pleasing to the senses but not to the spirit. Only Jesus can feed the soul and bring spiritual fulfillment.

THE FLATTERY OF TEMPTATION

Everyone wants to feel special. Most enjoy a sincere compliment now and then. A word of affirmation, a note of appreciation, or a look of admiration can make us feel important. Let's face it. Most of us like to be liked.

Satan knows this and uses it to his advantage. Like her master, the adulterous gains control through flattery, "So I came out to meet you; I looked for you and have found you ... With persuasive words she led him astray; she seduced him with her smooth talk," (Proverbs 7:15 and 21). Three times in verse 15 this temptress says, "you," making it evident she specifically sought out this particular young man.

Hogwash! Not to be crude, but do you really think this prostitute cared who she slept with? No. She cared about one thing, and it wasn't her client; it was getting paid. But that's not very flattering, not to the young man. So she puffed up the lad, making him feel special; because flattery is an effective tool in getting what she wants. How often has temptation used flattery to snare its prey?

- *"You deserve better than her!"*
- *"They don't appreciate your talents!"*
- *"You could do a better job than him!"*
- *"Skim a little they don't pay you enough anyway!"*
- *"They deserve what they get for what they did to you!"*

All of these implying how wonderful and amazing we are, amazing enough to excuse our sin. But temptation boosts us only to knock us down; building our egos to enjoy a laugh at our expense. Romans 16:18 tells us, "And by their smooth and flattering speech they deceive the hearts of the unsuspecting." In agreement Proverbs 29:5 reveals, "Whoever flatters his neighbor is spreading a net for his feet." Beware of anything that puffs you up and tells you how great you are. Temptation likes to blow up a balloon, simply to pop it!

Fact and Fiction … Reality can rarely compete with fantasy. And masqueraded beauty never discloses everything behind the mask. Our expectations and imaginations often leave those we love at a huge disadvantage. It is absolute foolishness to fall for a love that's not real at the expense of a love that is. Remember the next time you are tempted to find greener pastures, the grass may be greener but it's just as hard to mow.

THE FAKERY OF TEMPTATION

After the flattery, temptation is revealed as a phony, offering a gift it is incapable of bestowing. "Come, let's drink deep of *love till* morning; let's enjoy ourselves with *love,*" she coolly offers to the young man (Proverbs 7:18 emphasis mine).

This seductress doesn't promise sex or mere physical pleasure; she promises a whole lot more – She promises love. A quick comparison of Proverb 7 and I Corinthians 13:4-8 illuminates that Temptation is promising something it cannot deliver. For, "Love is patient, love is kind. It does not envy, it does not boast, it is not proud. It is not rude, it is not self-seeking, it is not easily angered, it keeps no record of wrongs. Love does not delight in evil but rejoices with the truth. It always protects, always trusts, always hopes, always perseveres. Love never fails."

This is not what she offers our young friend. Temptation can give none of what love promises. It is a fake. Temptation never offers what it really possesses, only a cheap imitation and a sour after taste.

In the Garden, Eve took the fruit because the Tempter promised, "When you eat it ... you will be like God." (Genesis 3:5). She was sold a bill of half truths and swallowed it whole. The serpent said she wouldn't die, while under his breath he whispered, "Not yet anyway ... and not the way you think."

> *"'Hey, look over here! I've got something you really want. It tastes good, feels good, and is a lot more fun than your boring walk down the street. Come on in and take a look.' That's temptation, suggesting to your mind ways to serve yourself instead of God." – Neil T. Anderson from his book The Bondage Breakers*

Sin deceives us into believing that it's really as good as it looks, feels, or sounds. But it never is. Temptation *always* promises what it cannot deliver. A new life may sound good, but you won't find it in that direction, life is a promise only God can fulfill. Temptation promises life, but can only deliver death.

THE FRUIT OF TEMPTATION

While temptation's promises are shaky, its consequences are certain. "All at once he followed her like an ox going to the slaughter, like a deer stepping into a noose till an arrow pierces his liver, like a bird darting into a snare, little knowing it will cost him his life." (Proverbs 7:22-23)

The temptress promised him something she could not deliver and delivered something he did not want. Someone once said, "Sin will take you farther than you want to go, keep you longer than you want to stay, and cost you more than you want to pay." Temptation's attraction quickly fades when its fruit is produced; the rose of its beauty dissipates with the sting of its thorn.

"The brilliance of desire is far outmatched by the darkness of giving into it." Author Unknown[39]

I live in a land of hunters, Montana. Through these outdoorsmen I have learned an appreciation for the wild; and in the process discovered another lesson behind this passage.

While studying Proverbs with a group of students, one such marksman posed a question I had never asked, "Why does the Bible say he was shot in the liver and not the heart?" he inquired. I was curious, and confused, so I urged him to continue. "By shooting the deer in the heart," he explained, "You would kill the animal faster. Shooting it in the liver would kill it, but it would suffer for hours before it eventually died."

Then it dawned on me. The Devil doesn't just want to destroy – no that would never satisfy his vengeful hatred. He wants more. He wants pain, wrenching screams, tears of hopelessness; to see our very souls squirm and tremble under the shaft of his piercing bolt. Prolonged pain and a slow agonizing death, this is his aim.

Look into the eyes of those who have fallen for the seductive call, unable to find grace. The misery in a young girl's eyes whose innocence is lost, the slurs and staggers of a man hopelessly addicted to alcohol, the hope drained from the child that no one seems to want. Then look in the mirror, as I have, and see the pain in your own face. For we've darkened her doorway, and bare the scars of an arrow intent on our misery.

We're not alone, "*Many* are the victims she has brought down; her slain are a mighty throng." (Proverbs 7:26). Her trapped and tortured occupy a long list; all of humanity – except one. And he defeated temptation because of the weapon he chose.

A Side Note — Is it really that DANGEROUS?

Temptation: we play with it, coddle it, and peek at it from afar. It doesn't appear that harmful, it even seems inviting. Some temptation is so familiar and subtle that we no longer notice its approach. It becomes like that old friend, the one we know is a bad influence, but we're too comfortable with it to break the tie.

We take a little taste and dip our toe into its tranquil waters not knowing that a terrible monster waits under the surface, waiting for our final plunge. We just don't take it seriously; unwilling to believe something that feels so good could be so wrong. But this stuff can kill! Its goal is complete domination.

Temptation, like its author, only has one desire: to kill, steal and destroy. It will give the sweet taste of the apple, only to destroy with the poison; the offer of momentary pleasure, to rejoice in the pain that follows. Underestimate this enemy and it could cost you everything.

REDISCOVERING YOUR ADVANTAGE

Our fight against temptation is a battle we can win! At the very beginning of this Proverb we learn the secret to victory. "My son, keep my *words* and store up my *commands* within you. Keep my *commands* and you will live; guard my *teachings* as the apple of your eye. Bind them on your fingers; write them on the tablet of your heart. Say to *wisdom*, "You are my sister," and call *understanding* your kinsman; *they will keep you from the adulteress*," (Proverbs 7:1-5)

God's Word holds the power to destroy the arrows aimed at our souls; to silence the seductive call, "For it is the power of God for salvation" (Romans 1:16). The Bible provides a massive advantage over temptation. Paul described our weapon as having, "divine power to demolish strongholds." (2 Corinthians 10:4).The writer of Hebrews described the Word as, "living and active; sharper than any double-edged sword." (Hebrews 4:12).

Just owning a Bible isn't sufficient. The call from Solomon is to "keep ... guard ... bind ... and write it on your heart." He goes so far as to demand we make wisdom a close relative and frequent companion. This wisdom, understanding, and sound judgment are important in the fight against temptation. But they only come to the traveler who wields the Sword of the Spirit, which is the Word of God. If your blade is dull, your battle will be brief, and you will lose. A sharpened sword is useless.

Jesus beat temptation because he relied on this weapon and knew it well (see Matthew 4:1-11). When temptation came knocking Jesus struck back with a phrase full of power, "for it is written."

> *"You may have to fight a battle more than once to win."*
> *— former British Prime Minister Margaret Thatcher[40]*

Don't try to defeat temptation with your opinion, it has little authority. Don't attempt to beat it with will-power, you possess far too little for that. Using clever quotes and stories may impress others, but not him. To defeat temptation you must choose as Jesus did, to know and use the Word of God!

TOP 10 WAYS TO BEAT TEMPTATION ...

The Word of God is our first line of defense against temptation. But there are other practical tools for beating this enemy: Always go with your first line of defense (and offense) but if you need extra backup give one of these a try.

1. *Recognize it for what it is* — temptation is deadly. No matter how it looks it is not a friend, no matter how it feels it will always destroy in the end.
2. *Acknowledge the consequences, ignore the pleasure* — Too often we admire the enjoyment temptation offers and ignore the consequences. That is one of its greatest tactics – exaggerate the pleasure, underestimate the pain. By focusing on the consequences we avoid falling for a false fantasy.
3. *Don't fight Alone* — "As Iron sharpens iron so one man sharpens another" (Proverbs 27:17). To defeat temptation we are better equipped if we are not alone. We need others to

confide in, who will lovingly confront us if we make wrong choices.

4. *Know your weaknesses* — By knowing our weaknesses we can be better prepared for the attack. Then we can pray for God's help and deliverance. "Lead us not into temptation" (Matthew 5:13).

5. *Know Satan's Schemes* — "For we are not unaware of his schemes" (2 Corinthians 2:11), but sometimes we act like it. Satan has used the same temptations for thousands of years. He has no new tricks, because he doesn't need them; we keep falling for the old ones.

6. *Deal with it quickly* — James the brother of Jesus wrote that sin begins with a thought (James 1:14). So don't play with it. Get rid of it, rebuke it right away.

7. *Make sure it's dead* — Goliath lay dead from a rock sunk in his head but David decapitated him anyway ... WHY? Because he wanted his tormentor finished once and forever. Don't leave temptation any chance of resurrection. Get it out of your home, out of your heart, out of your hands and out of your head!

8. *Draw near to God* — Our hunger and pursuit of God vastly diminishes the influence temptation has over us. We become so enamored by one far more wonderful, that temptation looses much of its appeal. (see James 4:7 and 8)

9. *Get your rest* — People make dumb choices when they are sick, tired and burnt out. Make sure your body has what it needs and when it doesn't be aware of your vulnerability for, "Fatigue makes cowards of us all."

10. *Stay Away* — "He was going down the street near her corner, walking along in the direction of her house" (Proverbs 7:8). Walking straight into the trap. We can't avoid temptation but we don't have to go looking for it either. Mark Twain wrote of temptation, "It is easier to stay out then get out."[41]

ONE LAST THOUGHT ...

Sometimes fighting and arguing with temptation isn't the best option. Joseph did not argue the pros and cons with Potiphar's wife about her proposed sleeping arrangements. That would have solved nothing. As a man and a slave, her beauty, not to mention her ability to grant his freedom, might have eventually won him over. No, Joseph got out of temptation's company as fast as he could.

In contrast, Eve sat around, arguing with the Tempter. Too bad she didn't run too. Her error cost us all. Sometimes the best response to the seductive call of sin is a world-class sprint. When dealing with this formidable enemy the Bible almost always gives us a one word piece of advice. Flee!

Temptation is many things but one thing it is not is unbeatable. When sin makes its daily seductive suggestions, don't think, don't hesitate, don't wait one second, turn around as fast as you can ... and run.

> *"Every day in the African savanna a lion wakes up. He knows if he is going to survive he must outrun the slowest antelope. Every morning an antelope wakes up. He knows if he is going to survive he must outrun the fastest lion (or at least the slowest antelope!). In life, whether you are an antelope or a lion, when the sun comes up you better be running!"*[42]

TEMPTING QUESTIONS:

1. How can we battle the attractiveness of temptation? How can your relationship with God and others aid in this battle?

2. Have you witnessed temptations aggressiveness and sneaky ways of working? How can we be better prepared?

3. Do you see temptation as an enemy out to destroy you and everyone you love? How will this help you the next time it comes knocking?

4. What temptations hound you? How will you protect yourself? Are there things you need to get rid of or things you
   need to avoid?

5. Read Proverbs 24:11 and 12. How might God have us
   respond when we see others falling into temptation's trap?

Stop #9

MIRACULOUS MOMENTS IN THE MIDST OF THE MUNDANE

The audacity of some people! Making you pay a bill again after you already paid it last month. Who do loaning institutions, the power company, and telecommunication corporations think they are? And how about your car? Ever been forced to fill up the tank only weeks or even days after your last visit to the pump? It may be frustrating, but that's life. We do something once, and then do it again … and again, and again?

Life tends to run in cycles. We wake up, hit the snooze bar a few times, get out of bed, take a shower, brush our hair and comb our teeth (on those rough mornings), grab a bite for breakfast and run out the door to the office. When we get there we do whatever it is we're paid to do, usually somewhat of the same thing every week. We drive home in some form of traffic and pull into the driveway. We open the door say, "I'm home," and hope that someone cares enough to come running. Then we plop down watch the news, eat some dinner, spend a little quality time with the family (and/or the TV), go to bed, and wake the next morning to do it all over again.

Homemakers experience this same frustration. Clothes washed, clothes dirtied (and often left on the floor). Meals made, meals eaten. Dishes soaked, dishes soiled. House cleaned, house demolished. The cycle goes on and on and on, until someone learns to pick up after themselves.

> *"It's not true that life is one thing after another – it's one thing over and over." Edna St. Vincent Millay*[43]

Sound like fun? Probably not, but vaguely familiar? Maybe just a little. Now I'm not trying to bash routine. It can be comfortable, familiar and that's not all bad! However this kind of life can feel a bit mundane even boring at times. And none of us set out to live life bored; doing the exact same thing over and over and over again – forever!

We hope for more; a dream come true, something miraculous. But most of life looks far from supernatural. We compare ourselves to those who walked with Jesus, or others who trod the paths of the book of Acts, or witnessed the mighty wonders in the Old Testament and wonder – Is this it? Jesus said, "Anyone who has faith in me ... will do even greater things than these," (John 14:12) but paying the bills on time and getting the kids to school doesn't quite compare.

SUPERNATURAL MOMENTS IN SCRIPTURE

There's no question many in scripture experienced the supernatural. But take another look and you'll discover another fact. For the most part, these individuals lived rather ordinary and yes, even mundane lives before, and even after, their "God encounter." We remember their Big Day yet often forget about the hundreds of plain Jane days that surrounded them.

Observe Jacob lying on a rock in the middle of the wilderness. It seems lying is what he's best at. He's running for his life and looking for a wife, but otherwise his greatest moments include making stew and taking blessings (not to mention becoming the first person to commit identity theft). Fleeing Esau's wrath, Stew Boy stops to camp for the night. As he rests on his rocky bed an out-of-this-world event occurs. The angelic host put on quite a show and God gives Jacob a failsafe guarantee, "I am with you" (Genesis 28:15).

Who could forget Moses at the Red Sea? God holds up the water, sends fire down from heaven, then drowns the greatest army of that day. Now that's something supernatural. But what about the 40 years Moses spent in the shadow of Sinai parting sheep? And another 40 years as a prince in Pharaoh's household? And after the Exodus, he wandered in the wilderness with a million people for another 4 decades. A large part of his 120 years was spent in the palace, in the pasture, or conducting funerals for the millions who died in the dessert. Sure he had his excitement, but it was all in the midst of many mundane, tedious tasks.

A glance at the life of our Lord provides similar insight. Jesus lived a little over 33 years, yet for the majority of that time did no miracles. His first recorded miracle was done after he reached his thirtieth birthday, at a country wedding no less, with few witnesses. In fact 18 years of his life are described in these words, "And he grew in wisdom and stature and in favor with God and man."(Luke 2:52). Sure that's a great thing to note, but it's still not very miraculous. It seems well, pretty ordinary.

The miraculous moments grow in the midst of the mundane. The supernatural interrupts the lives of each of us – as God determines. We walk out the process that is necessary to fulfill our purpose, taking the journey God sets before us. Then on the way in all of our plodding and pushing through, God shows up with a moment beyond our wildest dreams.

That's how it happened to the people in scripture. On the way to where they were headed God interrupted their journey with a miracle. They did their thing and in the mundane moment turned miraculous, God did His.

- Gideon in a wine press threshing grain, drafted to lead one of the most unlikely victories in the history of mankind; 300 men vanquished an army too vast to number (Judges 6-7).
- Samuel on his way to dreamland heard God's call, beginning a life of service and intimacy with Him (I Samuel 3).
- David, leading sheep in the fields, crowned King and Shepherd of God's people (1 Samuel 16).

- Mary of Nazareth striving to live out her teenage years, pronounced as God's chosen mother to give birth to the Savior of the World (Luke 1).
- Peter, Andrew, James and John came home from a bad day of fishing only to have one of their greatest catches because they heeded the advice of a carpenter (Luke 5).
- Phillip walking along a desert road runs into a high ranking Ethiopian official. He shares some insight and the hope found in Christ, launching the gospel into un-reached Africa (Acts 8).

"Anyone who doesn't believe in miracles isn't a realist"
— David Ben-Gurion, late prime minister of Israel[44]

The list seems endless and the truth timeless; God loves to turn an ordinary day into an extraordinary moment – to do the miraculous in the midst of the mundane. In the light of this, how should we live? The next few pages help answer that question.

BEWARE OF SEEKING SIGNS

Miracles attract attention. People desire the whispers of another world yet often prefer the explosions. As a pastor I have watched too many church members leave to find signs; to witness the "supernatural" somewhere else.

In the 1990's many in the church in America hungered for the miraculous. Often these epicenters of activity were called revivals and named after the cities in which they originated. People were drawn to these places, excited to see something out of the ordinary.

News of laughing, jumping, and barking floated down from the north while in the south word spread of crying, falling, and shaking. All over the nation, it seemed, little pockets of prolonged such events were popping up. People flocked to these churches and cities to witness the commotion, hoping to take revival home with them.

Now my intentions here are neither to verify nor vilify these events. I believe that during this time many people came to faith in

Christ and miracles did occur. I am far too finite and limited in my knowledge to criticize.

But one thing these years taught me was this; sign seeking will never replace consistent walking. And trading the latter for the former presents soul crippling dangers. How could seeking after signs be dangerous?

Trading the Savior for a Sign — When we seek after signs alone, we do not seek the Savior. We look for a miraculous hand out, but seek not to maintain a heart permanently altered by the Maker. Jesus puts it this way, "A wicked and adulterous generation asks for a sign." (Matthew 12:29 and 16:4). Many in Jesus' day wanted the Nazarene to touch their bodies but most did not open up their souls. Their amazement at what he did turned into anger at what he said.

His disciples faced similar results. In Acts chapter 8, Simon the Sorcerer, a man accustomed to amazing people with his black magic and trickery, believed Phillip's message. But when Peter arrived and touched the people resulting in the baptism in the Holy Spirit, Simons deeper desire surfaced. He wanted power.

Simon offered Peter money and in return Peter offered him a piece of his mind, "May your money perish with you … your heart is not right before God. Repent of your wickedness and pray to the Lord. Perhaps he will forgive you for having such a thought in your heart. For I see that you are full of bitterness and captive to sin" (Acts 8:20-23).

Craving what God gives more than God is spiritual adultery. We show that our hearts are wicked and betray the Giver with the very gifts he offers.

The Sinister Side of the Supernatural — Running after signs opens the door to deception. Those who desire power more than truth, trade absolutes for experience. And faith based solely upon experience is dangerous. In no time flat, you can slip from honest seeker of Christ to the entrapments of New Age philosophy, cults, and even the Occult.

Satan is a master counterfeiter, who "masquerades as an angel of light" (2 Corinthians 11:14). And he's good at it. Good enough to, "deceive even the elect –if that were possible" (Matthew 24:24). Like the Egyptian sorcerers and magicians who squared off with

Moses, Satan can produce exact replicas of the miraculous (Exodus 7).

But he cannot copy the truth. He is incapable of such an act; for he is the father of lies. Signs alone are an incomplete demonstration of what is right.We must rely on truth; trusting only in experiences supported by God's Word.

Hopping out of the Father's Plan and into the Fire — Many have felt the guiding hand of God only to turn from his will to follow a loader voice. Their church doesn't feel a certain way or they've found a livelier preacher, so they jump. God's will is tossed from the equation for a new sign to seek. Sign seeking can cause us to leave our commitments, to chase something more impressive to our senses.

Yet when signs fade and failures become exposed, "Hoppers" move on again. Jumping out of one situation and into another, always looking for a new thing.

Leaving a current situation to seek signs often proves to be the wrong decision. Perhaps we're planted to be molded, perhaps to make a difference in the lives of those around us. Either way the purpose goes unfulfilled because we jumped from the Father's plan, out of His will, and into the fire. Breaking commitments and leaving in the midst of adversity is a poor habit. Setting a corrosive example for others.

Demanding signs as a substitute for Christ is dangerous. Those who travel this pathway often find themselves worshipping the gifts of God, falling for the counterfeits of the Enemy of God, or forsaking the will of God. We must be careful in our desire to see the supernatural that we do not substitute revelation for relationship.

Christian Superstition – Manufacturing the Miraculous — When signs are the focus, everything can be interpreted as a sign from God. My car didn't start so God is telling me not to go to work today. The neighbor's house number is 666 so they must be evil. I felt a pain in my stomach when I passed that business, so God must not want me to go there. All feelings become signs from God and we are directed by circumstances –applying our own interpretation.

God speaks to us in mysterious and unusual ways, but those who seek after signs interpret ordinary phases of life as supernatural directives. Maybe your car not starting had more to do with poor car maintenance then a miraculous message. Perhaps your neighbor's house number is nothing more than that, their house number. Maybe that stomach pain is caused by too much pizza and not divine intervention.

But it can grow worse. Some so eager to hear from God not only misconstrue and misinterpret ordinary events, they even go so far as to manufacture signs – giving God a little help by arranging events to fit a particular message. But God doesn't need our help to produce proof. If we manufacture signs to impress or direct others, it's no longer miraculous – it's manipulation; Christian superstition.

However, balance is important. Matthew 24, Luke 21, and Mark 13 all record Jesus' warnings regarding the signs of the End of the Age. Again and again he repeats "Watch out ... Be alert ... Be on your guard." In addition, God used signs to confirm his will with many. These included Abraham (Genesis 17), Hezekiah (2 Kings 20:9) Gideon (Judges 6:36), even the shepherds were told of the Messiah's birth, "And this shall be a sign unto you" (Luke 2:12).

Jesus reprimanded the Pharisees and Sadducees for not paying attention to signs, "You know how to interpret the appearance of the sky, but you cannot interpret the signs of the times" (Matthew 16:3). Yet, go one verse further, Jesus rebukes the generation who asks for a sign. Contradiction? I don't believe so. What Jesus is communicating is two separate situations. The first are those individuals who ignore God's clear message and the second are those who want God to do things their way. To give them the sign they want to see, so that they can use it as they see fit.

God can speak to us through signs. When he does we'd be wise to listen and obey. But we don't need to make them up — not every incident and event is a divine message.

EXPECT THE UNEXPECTED

Beware of the pendulum swing. One side of this coin is the exclusive seeking after miracles but the other extreme can be just as damaging. The fact that some misuse or become consumed by the pursuit to witness the supernatural does not nullify its existence. Nor does the counterfeit condemn the genuine article. In fact these truths only validate the reality of miracles, and the blessing God intends for them to be.

"Expect a miracle!" – Oral Roberts[45]

God makes no mistakes and only delivers good gifts. He wants us to enjoy the miracles he provides, to earnestly desire those moments when heaven touches earth. God wants us to live with expectancy.

Jesus often asked those who came to him, "What do you want me to do for you?" He wanted to know if they came to him with expectation. In the case of the mute, demon-possessed, or the dead, someone else came to Christ for them expecting a miracle. Others said nothing, but by their actions reached out to the Master.

Faith is a verb — it moves, motivates, and leads us to expect from the hand of God the unexpected. "Without faith it is impossible to please God, because anyone who comes to him must believe that he exists and that he rewards those who earnestly seek Him." (Hebrews 11:6).

In the book of Acts, a crippled man sat at the Gate Beautiful. Day in and day out he waited, begging for help. But this day was different. "When he saw Peter and John about to enter, he asked them for money. Peter looked straight at him, as did John. Then Peter said, 'Look at us!' So the man gave them his attention, *expecting* to get something from them."(Acts 3:3-4 emphasis mine).

Though he did not get what he expected, still he expected something. That is what often happens with miracles. We don't get what we expect, we get infinitely more. But the key is living in the expectant anticipation that God can do anything.

A while back I heard a story about a drought in a Midwest town. The situation was so dire the pastor of the small church called for a prayer meeting. To his surprise on the day of the vigil, his entire church was filled with people. The young minister walked up and down the aisles greeting many he had not seen for some time. As he rounded the pulpit and prepared to begin the call to prayer, he noticed a wonderful sight. There seated in the front row in a pretty pink dress sat a young girl. There was nothing extraordinary about this child except the possession that lay across her lap; a red umbrella. Tears filled the pastor's eyes. You see, everyone else came to pray for rain, but the little girl arrived expecting God to answer.[46]

Don't shy away from the miraculous, just don't make it your God. God wants us to believe and have faith that he is able to save, deliver, and heal. Over and over again Jesus instructed those around him to have faith. "If you have faith as small as a mustard seed you can say to this mountain, 'Move from here to there', and it will move. Nothing will be impossible for you." (Matthew 17:20).

"Look at the nations and watch and be utterly amazed.
For I am going to do something in your days that you
would not believe even if you were told."
Habakkuk 1:5

FOCUS ON THE UNSEEN

Where we place our focus in life determines our response to miracles. How do we maintain balance? Writing to the church at Corinth the Apostle Paul urged them to keep proper focus. "So we fix our eyes not on what is seen, but on what is unseen. For what is seen is temporary, but what is unseen is eternal." (2 Corinthians 4:16-18).

This past summer I spent over 60 hours planting grass seed in our front yard. A large amount of time for such a task, perhaps, but not when your property is a "rock farm." For weeks I raked and hacked at rocks trying to prepare the soil. Cool summer mornings turned to hot summer days as I fought to make the ground level with only a few hand tools.

Muscles ached, fingers bled, skin grew red and sweaty, but eventually the land was ready. As I sit in the cozy confines of my office at home, winter has set in and the seed has gone dormant.

So why do so much work? Why dedicate so much time? To be honest when I focused on the immensity of the task and its mundane nature I easily became discouraged, despondent, disheartened, distressed – I just didn't want to do it! But the answer to the question "why" is found in light of a different point of view.

When I thought of the hope of greener pastures, the replacement of gravel for green grass, the loss of lonely dirt piles for lush lawns, the raking became tolerable, the blisters became badges of honor, sore muscles made sense ... In fact it wasn't a pain anymore it became a purpose.

Seeing the mundane tasks with a new perspective made them a necessary step in my journey. And this is what the Apostle Paul is attempting to open our eyes to. If we focus on the temporary we lose heart and become weary. And weariness is the entry way for apathy. So Paul exhorts us to focus on that which is unseen.

But think about what Paul is saying; fix your eyes on the unseen. Taste what you cannot eat; lean on what you cannot touch, listen to what you cannot hear; set your vision on what is out of view. Does that make any sense? Only if you walk by faith viewing life through Heaven's eyes! "Now faith is being sure of what we hope for and certain of what we do not see.This is what the ancients were commended for." (Hebrews 11:1-2).

"Faith is the bird that feels the light and sings to greet the dawn while it is still dark" James Hewett[47]

Many Christians become discouraged in this race of life. We forget why and for Whom we are living. We focus on what we can evaluate with our 5 senses and trust in their analysis. But there is much more to life than what our senses can reveal. Our focus point is clear, "Let us fix our eyes on Jesus, the author and perfecter of our faith" (Hebrews 12:2). Behind everything we see there is another world.

FOLLOW THE EXAMPLE OF THE FAITHFUL ... FAITHFUL IN THE SEEN

It is crucial that we keep our focus upon God. But there is a balance. Let's revisit my lawn prepping experience.

If all I did was dream about a lawn, focusing on what it might be like to play with my son in the grass, to enjoy picnics on the bountiful emerald carpet, envisioning the pleasure I will gain from gazing at the beautiful sage fairway ... *but never do a thing about it?* Then my dream would never be reality. The unseen would forever remain just that, unseen. Part of faith is faithfulness. Part of belief is action.

In Matthew chapter 25, Jesus tells us a parable of three workers who are given a financial trust. One was given five talents, a sum worth more than $5,000.00, another two talents, and still another one. Upon his return the master called his servants to give an account of his money. The first two doubled the funds entrusted, gaining wealth and position, while the third hid his away, gaining nothing, and was punished for his laziness.

This parable is a keen reminder of how high our God regards faithfulness. Notice that it was not the amount that each started with that made them different. Nor was it what they did with what they were given. We're really not sure what the first two did to make such a profit. Verse 15 reveals the Master only gave them what he knew each could handle, "each according to his ability." So what differentiated these men? Two did *something* and one did *nothing*.

We do not decide which gifts, abilities, talents, and resources we are given. We do not choose our families, dispositions, personality traits, or physical and mental capacities. We do not select our strengths and weaknesses or spiritual gifting. Much that makes us who we are was given and passed down. But what we choose to do with it is what counts. This separates those who receive the blessing from those who get the boot.

Pastoring in Montana I had the distinct privilege of working in the same state as Pastor Rich Skerbitz. Rich was the youth pastor in the small town of Shelby. The uniqueness of Rich is not found in his many abilities, rather what he has done with them.

You see, Rich, is physically handicapped, dependent upon a wheelchair. But that description doesn't seem to do Rich's situation justice. It is true he is unable to get around like most, but it's not due to a lack of effort. Rich Skerbitz has no legs and only one arm. He was born that way, living like this all of his life.

His father served in Vietnam and was exposed to agent orange (a chemical used to destroy vegetation to unearth hidden enemy). Rich could have spent his life agonizing over the state in which he was born. Yet instead, Rich Skerbitz lives out his talents impacting the young lives of those who attended his youth group; and I dare say, all who have come in contact with this man of God and hear his inspiring story. Rich may not be able to do the things others do the way they do them, but in God's sight he is capable of doing so much more.

We don't choose many things about our circumstances and situations, but we do choose to be faithful. How can we expect God to provide for us the miraculous when He cannot trust us with the mundane? The master, put his servants, "in charge of many things," only after they had proven to be faithful with "few things" (Matthew 25:21 and 23).

NOT EVERY DAY, BUT ALWAYS EXPECTANT

As I write these final words my home displays the fine touches of a wonderful seasonal transformation. The clock approaches 1 a.m. and my wife and son both lay nestled and snug in their beds. I'm sure what dances in their heads will cost more than a few sugar plums.

"If they were happening everyday they wouldn't be called miracles, they'd be called regulars." – Gary Richmond[48]

I love Christmas. So, why not celebrate this wonderful day more often? How about once a month, or even once a week? Simply stated, Christmas just wouldn't be the same. With the special quality and unique emotions lost, once a week Christmases would become mundane. Miracles are the same. If they occurred every day, miracles would be "normals" – the supernatural touch of God, routine.

The fact Christmas comes but once a year never tempers the excitement. It can't stop my nine year old from beginning next year's list only weeks after Christmas' passing. We can't live for this one day alone, yet we still live with expectancy. For even though it doesn't happen every day … it does happen. Christmas comes; and so do miracles.

SPECULATIONS ON THE SUPERNATURAL:

1. When it comes to seeking the supernatural balance can be difficult to maintain. In which area do you find yourself most often: Overly seeking or lacking expectancy? How might you change to gain a greater balance in your life?

2. Read 1 Corinthians 4:1-15. What possible assistance can these verses provide in helping us to focus on the unseen?

3. In what area might God be calling you to a greater level of faithfulness? How are you preparing the field of your life for the new growth of a miracle?

4. Sometimes we're either too busy or too forgetful to remember what God has done in our lives. What miracle has gone done in your life or the people around you? What prayers have He answered? Is there something you need to step out in faith for and believe again?

WRONG WAY OPPORTUNITIES – TRAP DOORS IN THE ROADWAY OF LIFE

I wonder if you've ever been guilty of the crime of the "short cut?" Behind the wheel of your vehicle, headed to some predetermined destination — yet still a little sketchy on some of the finer details — you soldier on, undaunted. With the determination of General George Patton you march forward at a brisk pace, "Always attack, never surrender, never retreat!" Winning the battle, by not stopping to ask for guidance, you lose the war — making record-breaking time ... in the wrong direction.

I must admit I've been found guilty of this infraction (bringing personal frustration and spousal friction). I seem to prefer continued activity over effective traveling, at least according to the evidence. As long as we keep going I'm happy. But motion and commotion don't always indicate correct navigational skills. In the pursuit of not wasting time to stop and ask, I've wasted greater amounts back tracking because my "short cut" led far out of the way and down a Wrong Way Opportunity.

Life is full of wrong turns; avenues with the illusion of accuracy and precision that transform our journey into a longer, more difficult process. Our own senses and emotions play tricks on our decision making, causing us to choose what we *think* or *feel* is right.

> **"I'd rather keep going than stop – even if it's in the wrong direction." Reverend Rick Ross[49]**

What at first cleverly disguises itself in the garments of opportunity can quickly degenerate, revealing an obstacle. God is not behind every opportunity. Some bumps in the road lift us up, while others make us fall. Some opportunities arrive Heaven-sent and others Devil delivered.

Like Simon Peter, the Lord may be calling you out into the deep waters of the unknown, or like Judas Iscariot, the Deceiver may be calling you to betrayal. Before we jump into any opportunity, we must make sure we know who is calling.

Wrong way roads can be difficult to recognize, because they don't always appear overtly or openly evil. Whereas the Back Alleys of Temptation offer obvious sin, wrong opportunities may appear good (or at least neutral) without explicitly asking us to disobey. These carnivores can only be recognized by those who are "aware of the devil's schemes" and alert to the possibility of traps (2 Corinthians 2:11). For these reasons they hold a subtle, dangerous quality that deceives many well meaning travelers.

I'm not the only one who plunges into life with the drive to arrive. Most of us have. From the rich to the poor, both princes and paupers, we've all raced toward our destination and fallen into a trapdoor in the road. It can happen to us all; no one is immune, not even a king.

A KING WHO PLAYED THE FOOL

There once was a mighty King who led his armies triumphantly into battle. He stood tall and strong, rugged and handsome. The people cheered his crowning and sang of his victories. With gallantry he defended his nation, reclaiming many lands once held by neighboring enemies.

After one such victory, the king recognized the enviable position he occupied. In his possession, chained and humiliated, stood a powerful ruler – a man of immeasurable worth – if used in just the right way. As he pondered the potential of his predicament, the

Potentate realized the imprisoned prince could prove priceless if his platoons were to continue to prevail (that was fun). In other words: The king assessed the situation and spared his captive's life planning to use him as an advisor or valuable hostage.

In addition, the richness of the land was notable and the food supply vast. The King's men, tired from the conflict, deserved a feast. A celebration would refresh his troops and raise morale, not to mention the impact on the King's popularity.

Seizing the opportunity, he shrewdly decided to distribute the food. He seized the plunder providing needed funds to continue the expansion of the empire. The plan was sound and the directives would be popular, the opportunity could not be passed up. Only one problem – the King was wrong!

The story may sound familiar, probably because you've heard it before. It's found in I Samuel chapter 15 and the King's name was Saul. Now, the right choice seems obvious to us, we already know the ending. But with a different perspective we discover hidden wisdom beneath Saul's actions— it's just not God's. It made sense to take a captive, to strengthen his armies with provision, to enrich the treasuries in preparation for the future. But Saul was still wrong. The King fell victim to the crime of the short cut and as punishment lost his kingdom.

We too have much to lose in the short cuts of life. Through Saul's choices we discover the signs of wrong-way opportunities that come one the way. And a warning to the destination driven to go back before it's too late.

"There is a way that seems right to a man but in the end it leads only to death." Proverbs 14:12

SIGNS OF A WRONG WAY

One way streets. Almost every city has them. You know them by their signs – "Do not enter," they shout in red, "One Way Only," they read in black and white, still others warn, "No left turn," "Wrong Way" or display a crossed out arrow instructing the more visual learner, which direction *not* to go. These signs are posted to insure the safety of all who travel.

I grew up in a town possessing a long stretch of one way streets. Most often the journey down these avenues remained pleasant for both driver and pedestrian. Yet occasionally a distracted motorist would ignore the warnings. Typically, only the misguided driver was impacted by this experience, learning a stressful lesson in paying attention. Yet a few times the unheeded signs had greater consequences, sometimes fatal.

Fortunately for us, God marks out the Wrong Way Opportunities with his own set of signs. Most often the signs aren't that hard to see – if we're looking.

Sign #1 ... Self-glorification

Saul was called by God, anointed to complete the mission to annihilate an evil enemy. He went as God's commander and for God's glory. But where do we find King Saul after the battle. Is he thanking God for the victory? Is he praying for the Lord's continual guidance? Is he leading his men in giving honor to God? The answer is no, no, and No! So what was our valiant king doing? Visiting Gilgal to "set up a monument in his own honor" (1Samuel 15:12).

Saul was granted grace by God and a second chance, and what does he do? He builds a statue to his own glory! Now, we don't build monuments for ourselves; no that would be too obvious. But perhaps there are times we act with, not entirely, selfless motives. "It's all for Gods glory," we say, but even that can be pride cloaked in humility.

Whenever motivation is even partially for self promotion, watch out. Even Jesus, "did not consider equality with God something to be grasped, but took on the form of a servant." (Philippians 2:5). When we seek glory for ourselves we cannot bring glory to God.

"None are so empty as those who are full of themselves"
– Benjamin Whichcote[50]

Saul was exalted to make God's name great, instead he sought his own greatness and chose to demonstrate his own wisdom. Saul pleased himself and his people, leaving God a distant third. Finding success he drowned in its seduction, but it wasn't always that way.

When Saul first became king he was "small in his own eyes" (1 Samuel 15:17). On the day of his introduction, he hid from the glory and responsibility (1 Samuel 10:21-23). Saul started strong, but didn't finish that way. Like the man who foolishly built his house on the sand, the kingdom of Saul came crashing down all around him. He had forgotten there is only one King

In 1717 when France's Louis XIV died, his body was placed in a golden coffin. He called himself the "Sun King", and his court was the most magnificent in Europe. To dramatize his greatness, he gave orders that during his funeral the cathedral would be dimly lit with a solitary candle set above the coffin. As thousands waited in hushed silence, Bishop Massilon began to speak. Then slowly reaching down and snuffed out the candle and solemnly said, "Only God is great!"[51]

Jesus warned, "Everyone who exalts himself will be humbled, and he who humbles himself will be exalted." (Luke 18:14). All of our candles will be snuffed out one day. The only ones who will matter are those who live to display God's glory. All other kingdoms will fall, all other paths are Wrong Way Opportunities.

Sign #2 ... Self-deception

Saul's wrong way began with a monument, but that was only the beginning. In his hast to honor himself he missed another sign. He was also fooling himself.

When Samuel finally locates the self-absorbed statue maker, Saul reports great news. "The Lord bless you, I have carried out the Lord's instructions.'" Samuel gives Saul a puzzled look and asks, "What then is the bleating of sheep in my ears? What is this lowing of cattle that I hear?" But the king continues with his defense, pleading his case, even though wrong, "I did obey the Lord ... I went on the mission the Lord assigned me. I completely destroyed the Amalekites and brought back Agag their king." (1 Samuel 15:13-14, 20-21)

Agag lived? God's commands included the death of King Agag, yet the wicked king lived, with Saul's full knowledge and protection. In his disobedience King Saul actually becomes a protector to the enemy of God. He even attempts to lure Samuel into believing his lies, only admitting fault after the revelation of the consequences.

"The man who knows the truth and has the opportunity to tell it, but who nonetheless refuses to, is among the most shameful of all creatures." — Theodore Roosevelt[52]

Hiding from the truth through self-deception is sign number two. We deceive ourselves, justifying our actions, believing it's really not so bad. We use excuses, anger, deception, compromise, hiding behind something or someone else, or just plain ignoring it – but none of these tactics work.

King Saul slipped up when he began to think! His "thinking" convinced him he knew best, not God, but none of us possess such wisdom. Even if the benefits of the opportunity are debatable, it matters little if it's not God's will. We can pray and seek for some opportunity that we think best, but God knows it will hinder his blessing. Self deception always runs counter to God's will and His Word, count on it.

Sign #3 ... Playing the Blame Game

Excuses, pride, deception ... what would Saul try next? How about shifting the blame. Saul stops denying his actions, but instead of taking full responsibility he tells Samuel, it's really not his fault. He gives the prophet his best puppy dog eyes, and explains, "The soldiers brought them from the Amalekites; they spared the best of the sheep ... I was afraid of the people so I gave into them." (1 Samuel 15:15 and 24).

Wrong ways are littered with the bones of those who could not accept responsibility for their actions. If you look closely at the remains, you will notice a major section of the skeletal structure missing. They have no backbone. Adam blamed Eve, and we've been using it ever sense. We may believe that God actually buys our shifting of the blame and inability to do what's right, but he doesn't.

> *"He who conceals his sin does not prosper, but whoever confesses and renounces his sin finds mercy." —*
> *Proverbs 28:13*

Who was the King of Israel anyway? Was it not Saul? Was he not responsible for the conduct of his men? Could he not stop what they were doing if he really wanted to? Just hours before he was setting up a statue to declare his greatness and now the "great king" can't even enforce a simple command among his troops. Saul blamed the soldiers for the animals that lived, but what about Agag?

By pointing out the sins of others Saul attempted to distract Samuel from his own. It is so much easier to blame others than to deal with me; to refuse to take responsibility for my actions because somehow mine aren't as bad compared to theirs. But when you start playing the "Blame Game," look down at the road your on, it's a Wrong Way Opportunity.

Sign #4 ...Token obedience

Let's give Saul a break for a moment. After all, it wasn't as if he completely disobeyed; he did kill and destroy a great deal, following *the majority* of God's instructions. His own words indicate how close he came, "They spared the best of the sheep and cattle to sacrifice to the Lord your God, *but we totally destroyed the rest.*" (1 Samuel 15:15 emphasis mine). Saul obeyed, while not "completely," perhaps "mostly." In school seventy percent still passes, in baseball a .400 hitter is a star, in golf par is pretty good – but when it comes to obedience to God, "sort of" just won't cut it. Token obedience never does.

Saul hoped to hide behind the veil of good intentions. The animals were spared to sacrifice to the Lord and the food to strengthen the men, certainly God would understand. But God saw right through the token, to the heart.

When we stray the wrong way we often offer God some semblance of obedience. It makes us feel better, even if we're not. "Well," we think to ourselves, "I know God wants me to give 10% but maybe 5% will be OK." We justify, "I should pray and read the Bible but I'm busy." "I would never cheat on my wife; it's only pictures, just a little entertainment," we reason. "I'm not hurting anyone … All the other guys tried it … Its only one taste, hit, drink, shot … It's not gossip, if you mean well." On we go offering token obedience that is only a fair disguise for sin.

In our recent travels my wife and I met a young woman engaged to be married. She asked us questions about our wedding, marriage and family then she asked me what I did for a living. I confessed I was a pastor (you'd be surprised at the reactions of people to this answer). She responded with her own confession; she was a Christian. But then, for some reason, the conversation became more forced, awkward.

It seemed natural to ask her about her own relationship. She didn't seem as eager to talk. Then with hesitation she explained, "The old fashion way just doesn't work anymore." She continued, "You need to live with someone for a while before marrying … to work out the kinks."

My wife and I listened intently. We could not agree with her, yet at the same time didn't want to come off judgmental. Before we left the woman informed us of a spiritual sacrifice she and her future husband were making. In honor of Lent the entire family planned to abstain from eating fast food. She was proud of her willingness to give up something for her Religion.

How often do God's people choose to sacrifice something to the Lord, only to deny him the very thing He asked for? He commands us and we make bargains. But our self chosen sacrifices mean nothing when we take from him that which he sets aside as his own.

Jesus confronted the Religious leaders because of a similar *sacrificial disobedience*. He revealed their token obedience when he said, "You clean the outside of the cup and dish, but inside (you) are full of greed and self-indulgence …" (Matthew 23:24)

It seems the more religious we become the better we are at getting around God's commands. Religion alone helps us find the loop holes in the Law instead of following its intent. Yet, we do not face a God easily confused, manipulated, or mocked …"Do not be deceived: God cannot be mocked, A man reaps what he sows." (Galatians 6:7). Anything less than absolute obedience is absolute disobedience. Anything less than absolute truth is an absolute deception.

> *"Does the Lord delight in burnt offerings and sacrifices*
> *as much as in obeying the voice of the Lord? To obey is*
> *better than sacrifice." — 1 Samuel 15:22*

Sign #5 … Spiritual Separation

Of all the signs this may be the most tragic. Three times in Saul's conversation with Samuel he uses the phrase, "the lord *your* God." Saul refers to the God who chose him, anointed him, and called him not as *my God*, but as *Samuel's God*. What a sad commentary. In the midst of the pride, deception, irresponsibility, and token obedience, lays the greatest loss that Saul could ever imagine - and he didn't even recognize it.

Saul's King had been dethroned, replaced by a lesser god; a god of self. Half-hearted religion and selfish ambition supplanted his intimate relationship with Jehovah (see 1 Samuel 10:6-10).

When we choose Wrong Way Opportunities, the One we intended to serve is someone else's responsibility; someone else's friend. But there is hope.

Had Saul truly repented he would have found mercy. God hates spiritual separation – the Cross reveals to us what lengths He will go to get us back. We only need to drop the delusions and come home. As the glorified Christ pleaded with the church at Ephesus, so we must remember the height from which we have fallen, repent and return to God (Revelation 2:5). It's the only way to recapture our first love; to heal spiritual separation.

Sign #6 ... Reputation over Reality

After being "found out," rebuked, and sentenced, Saul reveals the true commitment of his heart. "Saul replied, 'I have sinned but please honor me before the elders of my people and before Israel.'" (1 Samuel 15:30).

Samuel ripped apart Saul's excuses and tore his charade to shreds. He pronounced God's rejection and judgment upon Saul's kingship and shamed his hollow attempts at appeasing the Lord. And all Saul cared about was *how he looked*. He asked for honor and public recognition — not forgiveness.

How others *thought* of him took priority over what God *knew* about him — illusion above truth, reputation over reality. Saul wanted people to think he was good even though he wasn't. In fact, through this whole incident the only one he ever asks to forgive him is Samuel, not God (1 Samuel 15:25). What a contrast to the next King of Israel.

David wept over his sin crying, "Against you (God) and you only have I sinned and done evil in your sight." (Psalms 51:4). But not King Saul, the Wrong Way Opportunity he took, had taken him – Hook, line, and sinker.

Saul kept the deception going to the very end. Only those closest to him witnessed the rapid deterioration. Saul got what he asked for, the honor and praise of men, and in the end it made him shallow, sickly, and bitter. And when a young musically talented shepherd boy walked into his life, things unraveled. Not because the boy was hateful or disloyal, but because he loved the God Saul rejected.

Saul settled for the appearance of a sterling reputation instead of a repaired reality. If we only pretend to be His, our efforts to mask the truth won't fool God. One day they will be exposed.

*"Man looks on the outward appearance, but the Lord
looks at the heart." 1 Samuel 16:7*

Sign #7 ... Divinely Passed By

One final sign peers through the fog of the King's foolishness.
Consider his climatic defeat, voiced by Samuel. "You rejected the
word of the Lord and the Lord has rejected you as king over Israel
... The Lord has torn the kingdom of Israel from you today." (1
Samuel 15:26 and 28)

King Saul's constant decisions toward Wrong Way Opportunities
led him to a dead end. God was done with him; done speaking to
him, done recognizing him, and done using him. Though years
would pass before Saul's death, as far as God was concerned, Saul
was finished.

We risk our usefulness in God's service when we walk as King
Saul did (not to mention the eternal consequences). The day Saul
spared a wicked king he lost everything, the cattle he saved cost him
the kingdom.

Jesus once asked, "What good is it for a man to gain the whole
world, yet forfeit his own soul?" (Mark 8:36) Perhaps King Saul
could best answer this question. I pray we will never be qualified to
do the same.

GUIDANCE FOR FACING OPPORTUNITIES

At times the signs aren't as clear as in the life of Saul.
Opportunities don't always appear bad or good. Sometimes we just
don't know how to respond to an open door because we're uncertain
who is speaking to us and guiding our desires.

We close our look at wrong way opportunities with a few suggestions to aid in deciphering what opportunities to take and which to
leave behind.

"Ask and it will be given to you; seek and you will find; knock and the door will be opened to you." – Matthew 7:7

Pray — This sounds simple enough, but how many decisions are made every day, without prayer. If we want to know the will of God, why not just ask him? He won't hide it from us, though he might wait to reveal it. James wrote, "If any of you lacks wisdom he should ask God, who gives generously." (James 1:5).

The hymn writer Joseph Scriven wrote, "Oh what peace we often forfeit, oh what needless pain we bare, all because we do not carry everything to God in prayer."[53] Remember Joshua before his defeat at Ai. He failed to pray and therefore failed to win. The opportunity became a trap because he did not ask. Many problems and pit falls can be avoided if we pray before we pursue.

Wait— Sometimes this can be a challenge, but it's a great way to minimize mistakes. Often I fight the desire to rush straight into action, seeing a problem and applying an instant solution. Yet, on a few occasions my haste produced more damage than assistance.

To temper this area of my personality God sent me to serve Pastors mastered in the art of patience. Through them I learned that God, not only possesses a right plan, but also a right time. Without waiting we do exactly the right thing at precisely the wrong moment.

Try waiting, it often produces wonderful results. "They that wait upon the Lord shall renew their strength, they shall mount up on wings like eagles, they shall run and not grow weary, they shall walk and not faint." (Isaiah 40:31 NKJV). The more desperate the need for an answer, the greater the need to wait.

"Our patience will achieve more than our force" – Edmund Burke[54]

Know God's Word and Follow it— Don't try and make tough decisions without first checking the instruction book. God's word can save us loads of time and worry. Within its pages lay most of the answers, we only need to look. However, knowing isn't enough, we must put it into practice.

King Saul knew God's will, he just chose to ignore it. Sometimes it's not really a matter of knowing, but heeding and following. When we discover His guidance, and we will, the real question is, do we have the courage to follow?

Seek Godly Council— King Saul was blessed with the gift of Samuel, given as a mentor and a godly counselor. Today, pastors, parents, friends, teachers, church leaders, books and much more, stand in our lives as wonderful resources, for wisdom and direction. When we face questions that need answers and decisions that need solutions, God will often use the counsel of his servants to guide our lives. As Solomon observed, "He who walks with the wise grows wise, but a companion of fools suffers harm." (Proverbs 13:20).

Obey what you already know — You may be wondering about God's plan for your life— most likely, you're right in the middle of it. We tend to stare eagerly into the future for some untouchable time or task, but often possess all we need here and now.

This is a good rule to follow: If you've heard nothing new, do nothing new – keep going. Though frustrated and unnerved, stick to the path. Perhaps you sense a change, yet feel unsure. Experience tells me this move may still be weeks, months, and even years away, so remain faithful. President Theodore Roosevelt said, "Better faithful than famous."[55] Remember, it is the *faithful* servant the Lord will welcome home.

> *"Your primary assignment becomes whatever God wants*
> *you to focus on at the particular phase in your journey …*
> *Be diligent. Don't treat as trivial what God is asking you*
> *to accomplish." – Angela Lougee*[56]

Do your homework – God gave us a brain for a reason. True, our own thinking can get us into trouble. Human understanding and logic are often faulty, but when renewed by the word of God and submitted to the Holy Spirit, the mind can be a pretty effective tool. So I suggest, in the process of finding your way through life's twist and turns, employ some common sense.

When faced with an opportunity consider the pros and cons, check things out. Don't act on emotions and do your homework.

Evaluate your talents, gifts, abilities, and experiences. How has God uniquely gifted you? What do you enjoy? Ask yourself the tough questions and search your motives. Don't put your full trust in your own understanding, but don't be afraid to use your mind either – it is a terrible thing to waste.

Trust God – Using our heads is a good plan, however our thoughts are no substitute for trust. Sometimes decisions look easy. The option between a steak and a happy meal, or a job making $200,000 a year and one that pays $20,000. The choice is obvious, right? Maybe, and then again maybe not. There comes a day when a decision must be based on faith and not our figuring.

This means we may be called into the unknown or the difficult. Saul was doubtful in circumstances beyond his control. He did what came naturally instead of what was difficult. When opportunities present themselves we cannot afford to be ruled by fear or familiarity. We must follow God and rely on his peace (see Philippians 4:6-7), trusting him to make our paths straight.

Think of God FIRST – The most important thing we must do when faced with opportunities is place God as our top priority. We need to look at every crossroad and ask, how will this impact His kingdom, His reputation, His people, and my relationship with Him? This means I dispose of my agenda.

King Saul's biggest problem was incomplete surrender. He let this "king thing" go to his head, holding a different agenda than his KING. But when you serve God, he comes first. Even Jesus said of his choices in life, "I do nothing on my own … For I always do what pleases (God)." (John 8:28-29). He put God first, even when his Father's plan cost him his life.

Thinking of God first directs our paths to interesting locations. Hosea married a prostitute, redeeming her even after she returned to her previous profession (Hosea 1:2-3). Ezekiel lay on the ground for 430 days as a living illustration to God's people (see Ezekiel 4:4-8).

Moses was called to free a nation using the destructive and overwhelming power of a shepherd's staff and a promise – given from a bush.

Naman, cursed with the uncleanness of leprosy, was instructed to bathe in the filthy Jordan River. And John the Baptist started a ministry in that same filthy water to prepare the way for the one who would cleanse away the filth of the world.

Ananias, a Christian in Damascus, received a vision to search out a man named Saul, the same man who came to arrest Damascus Christians.

All of these and more were told to go, be, or do something that didn't make sense at the time, but they trusted the Lord and obeyed anyway. Stutterers called to preach to the nations; cowards called to conquer mighty foes; uneducated instructing the elite.

What a way to travel ... certainly not dull. In the end they followed God's commands, and when all was said and done, the road map led the right way because it was the way God chose for them. Though it made little sense, they followed, because they thought of Him first.

THE PAIN OF GETTING TOO CLOSE

The first house my parents owned had a trap door precariously placed in the living room floor. At times my imagination got the best of me, especially at night. What monsters lurked in the dark recesses of the basement when the lights went out? Creatures that in the day hid timidly from the light, at bedtime possessed great courage and cunning. Any creak or squeak, threw my mind into overdrive.

No monster ever came up through the basement at night (not that I'm aware of anyway). But what I remember most about the trap door is what went down.

Now let me preface this in defense of my parents. We were told to stay away from the trap door; over and over again Mom and Dad commanded us to keep away. Mom asked Dad to build a barrier and if we had the money, I'm sure he would've (right, Dad?). In all fairness, it is almost impossible to build a barrier large enough to restrain the curiosity of little boys.

One day my brother and I made our way to the edge of the trap door. Now being the eldest, and good son, I stayed back. But my poor younger brother was a different sort, making his story much more painful than my own. I'm afraid David's adventurous spirit led him too close to the trap door. And moments later - down, down, down, to the basement floor below.

Now in spite of what he might say or believe, I did not push him. There is no evidence to prove otherwise and I stand exonerated from all charges. The point is, when it comes to trap doors in the roadways of life, these Wrong Way Opportunities, listen to those who know better, be cautious and when you see it for what it really is ... keep out!

OPTIONS FOR OPPORTUNITIES:

1. Have you ever known what God wanted you to do but you weren't so sure you wanted to do it, so you cut a deal? How did this "token obedience" work out? What has it taught you for future situations?

2. Have you ever used the "blame game" or comparisons to wiggle out of a wrong? How did this impact your relationship with God and others?

3. Sometimes it can be easy to mistake a good reputation for really being good. What possible problems could arise from falling for this pit fall? How can we know who we can trust if all we really see is the reputation?

4. Look at the signs once again. Do any of them look familiar to a situation or decision you are facing? Make sure you are certain of the opportunities origin before you jump in.

5. Apply the suggestions outlined for making right decisions about opportunities to a choice you need to make. Go through these steps before making a final decision and right down the guidance you receive. Which of these will you make a permanent part of your decision making process?

Stop #11

DIVINE DELAYS AND DETOURS

There I was, stranded on the side of Highway 15, thirty two years old and ignorant of how to change a flat tire. To my shame, I've never been great with cars, but my choices were limited. *"Well,"* I thought to myself, *"no better time to learn."*

So where do I begin? First things first ... discard the directions and plunge right in. I tried this course of action for several minutes making little progress. Finally, looking to make sure no one was watching, I picked up the directions and began to read. Of course, at that very moment a voice asked, "Do you need help?" Even though my pride said "NO," my desperation won out.

I turned to face a man dressed in tight biker's spandex, a helmet in one hand while he steadied his twelve-speed with the other. Quickly and with some thoroughness, he instructed me on the finer points of tire replacement. As we talked and set to work, another car stopped, then another.

The first truck stopped and three ladies spilled out to aid a stranded driver and his bicycled rescuer. They just happen to attend the church I was on staff at. A moment later and this unplanned meeting became an opportunity to pray with them and encourage each in a difficult day. All the while my "spandexed" Good Samaritan continued his work on my vehicle.

The next vehicle was driven by a girl from our youth group, who had not attended in several months. Our conversation became another unscheduled appointment to help a searching traveler back to the right path. Three meetings I did not have time for, God planned for me nonetheless.

> *"God is rarely in our plans. But he's always in our interruptions." – Mark Lowry*[57]

That was Tuesday. Friday my family and I set off for a week long road-trip westward bound. During the drive we talked about my recent flat tire induced delay. I joked how it would make a great start for this chapter. Then out of the corner of my eye I noticed a blinking light illuminating the dash board. Its warning cut through the conversation as it declared, "Service Engine Soon." No problem, probably just a loose wire. My wife studied the manual to confirm my lack of concern. Just in case we decided to make a quick detour into Ellensburg, Washington.

Seven hours and nearly $700.00 later we were back on the road again. My destination driven side giving way to the journey focused life. I told my wife I would finish this chapter immediately. We needed no further blessings or illustrations of divine delays and detours. Holding in her laughter she commented, "I can't wait till you start writing about the miraculous."

The roadways of life are fraught with delays and detours. And even though I eagerly finish these pages dedicated to their purpose and existence, I know I am not finished traveling through their bewildering avenues.

Detours and delays aren't dead ends, they're just "not yets;" and they all have a purpose. I meet them everywhere and often in my least convenient moments. They seem to pop up when I'm in the greatest hurry. Angela Lougee wrote, "Most of us don't see our waiting periods as God's ordained season. We become anxious and restless, we may think that we're wasting time, (but) there are many waiting periods on the journey to a fulfilled destiny."[58]

"If you are clear and confident about the destination, you can handle a few detours along the way." – Andy Stanley from his book Next Generation Leader

It's amazing how small things can test our Christianity. And perhaps that's exactly why they are there. In the stillness, God reminds us that life is a journey. He speaks to our souls with gentle questions, *"My child, have you ever thought perhaps these delays come from me …that in the midst of your rush I place these stops in your path for a reason? These, my son, are not for your frustration but for you fulfillment … they are divine appointments."* We see them as problems yet our Father desires them to be blessings; the gift of a silent pause.

WHY DELAYS AND DETOURS?

We all experience delays on the way, pausing our momentum and detouring our journey. We rarely like them and often question the need for such time wasters. *"Are we there yet?"* we plead with God, like impatient children in the back seat of a mini-van. But is the question all that important? If God put the delay or detour in our path there's no getting around it. Besides the journey focused understand the process, and more importantly trust the divine Guide.

We can of course insist on being irritated by the wait. We can fuss at those who share the journey with us, whine about not getting our way, complain how tired this delay is making us, but if we do we will miss God's purpose. We will miss what He wanted us to see, what he wanted us to learn, what he wanted to create in us on the way.

"Stop" is not always a bad thing to hear, especially when the Heavenly Driver is at the helm. So if you find yourself in these uncharted pathways listen and learn from those who've gone before. Within their lives we find the diamonds of delays and detours forged through the pressure of the unexpected — revealing our need for them now more than ever.

THE PATIENCE OF A PATRIARCH

To discern the will of God and avoid Wrong Way Opportunities we need patience. But patience will never be learned in our own timing, when life proceeds on schedule, according to our ways, directives, and preferences. When our journey goes as planned, when the road follows precisely as the charts dictate, patience is unneeded and unattainable. The only way to get it ... is to need it.

In 1996, my wife and I decided to add a member to our young family. What we thought to be a chance to love two handfuls of fur soon became an exercise in patience. At only eight inches and just a few pounds, our new puppy was a package full of mischief. The whole house was his personal potty. He chewed on everything, he yapped at everyone, and ran everywhere except where we told him to. The multi-colored shag carpet we once hated became a savior, hiding the multitudes of stains caused by Teddy's many body fluids.

He is nearly thirteen years old now and quite the different animal. He still makes messes from time to time, but those early days of puppy-raising detoured my character into the land of patience. A fact that my "human son" can be most grateful for.

Abraham may not have owned puppies, but as the ultimate Journeyman, he was brought often to this place of patience. His whole life traveled toward a destination he never fully reached. God promised Abraham, "I will make you into a great nation and I will bless you; I will make your name great ... and all peoples on earth will be blessed through you." (Genesis 12:2-3)

Wonderful promises indeed, but Abraham only heard about them, he never witnessed their fulfillment. He never saw the great nation God made of his seed; he never saw the whole world blessed through the baby born in Bethlehem.

In fact it took another 20 years before God even began to honor his word. Why would God take so much time to fulfill his promise to Abraham? There are many possibilities.

God was establishing his chosen people through Abraham. It was important they learned to trust God; to live by faith and believe that nothing was impossible for Him. Abraham needed to know that divine providence and not self effort would accomplish God's promises. They needed to gain something that has evaded men for millennia – Patience.

> *"Don't despise the events of life that work patience*
> *– things that cause you to have to 'wait well.' They are*
> *friends not enemies." — Joyce Meyers[59]*

Paul reminded the church in Rome, "The just shall live by faith!" (Romans 1:17). You cannot have faith without patience – It is the paddle that keeps the rowboat of our faith going. If we lose our patience in the rapids and on the rocks of life we won't stick with our beliefs. God in his loving kindness, places delays and detours in our journey so that we might learn patience. Hebrews points this out when it declares, "… faith is being sure of what we hope for and certain of what we do not see." (Hebrews 11:1). Such faith is patient – not seeing, not knowing, resting on hope alone.

THE PERSISTENCE OF AN AMPHIBIAN

Patience is being willing to wait; persistence is "waiting aggressively." Patience is enduring through struggle and hardships while persistence is pushing through them. Abraham was taught patience; to wait for God to fulfill his promise to do what Abraham could not.

Face it; apart from a miracle Sarah was incapable of having a child. No matter what Abraham did nothing would change the dilemma they faced. Some delays and detours teach us to wait while others teach us to keep at it.

Some 2000 years later Simeon spent his days in the temple watching for the promise Abraham waited for. He was told by God that he would not die until he beheld the Christ. Through the power of the Holy Spirit this devout man stood in the temple courts, daily waiting for the Messiah to be revealed (See Luke 2:25-28).

How long would we wait? How attentive would we watch? Every day Simeon went to the temple, listening for the Spirit's call.

He was patient, no doubt, but beyond the edge of waiting he had learned persistence.

Think for a moment. What if on the day of Jesus' dedication, Simeon decided to take the day off; to go see the country side; to catch up with friends and the news of Jerusalem? What if after all that patience he had stopped being persistent and gone and done something else?

But not Simeon. Patience took on the extra aggressive activity that makes persistence. David wrote of persistence when he said, "Wait for the Lord; be strong and take heart and wait for the Lord." (Psalms 27:14). This kind of waiting give God control but activates our effort and courage. Persistence is patience that just keeps going.

"Slow and steady wins the race." – Aesop's fable of The Tortoise and the Hare

At a local bookstore I recently visited a carton hung behind the cash register. It depicted a frog being swallowed by a pelican. Heading down the mouth of the bird, the amphibian reaches back and grabs the predator's throat with his two webbed feet. The caption below reads, "Never give up." Now that's persistence.

THE PERCEPTION OF THE QUIET PLACE

I have learned to be surrounded by voices yet still hear nothing. This is beneficial when I'm trying to read or write and distractions attempt to bombard me. However there is a drawback. At times, I employ this skill at the wrong moment and with the wrong people.

One day a parishioner was speaking with me about some subject I honestly wasn't very interested in. I nodded my head in feigned interest, adding an occasional "really" or interested "hmmm" for flavor, to appear thoughtful. But in truth I was zoning out, my mind was elsewhere. Her voice faded like the adults in the Charlie Brown television specials, a droning tone, "wah wah, wah wah, wah wah." Suddenly she stopped, breaking my silent reflection. Then locked her eyes onto mine and asked, "Are you listening?"

Now I must admit I was a bit shocked at the question. I adeptly pulled to my mouth the topic of discussion and the few last words. But it was of no use, I'd been caught. I apologized, and she forgave me (thanks Bev). And from that day forward I have endeavored to become a better listener; this embarrassing detour teaching me to really hear what people are saying.

Detours and delays provide the time we lack to hear the voice of others, and especially the voice of God.

- David heard the Voice blowing through the trees in the hills surrounding Bethlehem as he cared for his father's flocks. He heard the quiet whispers as he fled the sword of his father-in-law. The stillness inspired songs written in anguish, joy, sorrow, and praise.
- Moses heard His voice in the shadow of Mount Sinai and in the dessert of his soul. There God's voice became clear through a bush that did not burn. Exodus 3:3 uses the Hebrew word "cuwr" which means, "to turn off."[60] In this detour Moses first perceived the firm yet gentle voice he would so desperately need through the remainder of his journey.
- Paul heard this call on the roadside of humility and in the prison of persecution. This same voice would call him to plant churches and speak through him in the face of power, royalty, and even death.
- John the beloved saw His glory and heard His message in the lonely Roman outpost of Patmos. The voice brought to him wisdom for the churches of his day and prophetic wonders for tomorrow.

"It wasn't until God saw Moses turn aside that He pursued him by calling him by name." – John Bevere from his book <u>Drawing Near</u>

The voice that spoke to David, Moses, Paul, and John still speaks to the sensitive servant today. We just don't have time to listen. Jesus said, "He calls his own sheep by name and leads them out ... and his sheep follow him because *they know his voice.*" (John 10:3-4 emphasis mine).

Many times in life's journey we are unable to recognize the voice of our Shepherd, because we have either crowded it out or invested little time in communing with him. So in his mercy our Heavenly Father places delays and detours in the path so that we might gain proper perception – the ability to hear his voice.

THE PROVISION FOR THE FUTURE

Imagine what the disciples must have felt. Just days before their prospects appeared bleak: Their master was dead, one of their number betrayed him then committed suicide, the strongest of them denied even knowing him, and as for the rest of them, they all fled into the foggy Judean night like frightened mice.

But now the memory had faded away as a ghoulish nightmare passes with the first light of dawn. He was alive! Jesus had risen, just as he promised. Can you imagine the excitement, the purpose? The horrible night had passed and joy flushed back into their lives on resurrection morn.

As they walked along the road toward Mount Olivet their emotions must have been mixed; excitement and joy mingled with loss and sadness, eager anticipation tempered by the impending goodbye. Though their emotions were clouded their purpose was clear.

"What's that? What is he saying now? Did Jesus just say, 'Wait?' Wait? You've got to be joking! He wants us to Wait?!" You might imagine their surprise. They had renewed passion, fresh excitement, purpose and a mission and what does Jesus command? "Don't leave town … wait." (Acts 1:4)

If there was anything these men wanted to do it certainly wasn't waiting. They wanted to prove themselves, to make up for all they had done wrong, to put the failures behind and get back to the work … But Jesus tells them precisely what to do, "wait." So, wait they did, and they received an irreplaceable gift; the Holy Spirit.

God often detours our lives to places we need to see, people we need to meet, and provisions we must acquire for our journey. The

Disciples desperately needed supernatural power and boldness to follow the Great Commission. They would face obstacles, persecution, needs, and circumstances requiring wisdom and authority they did not possess alone. So they waited and God provided.

The Apostle Paul experienced a similar detour. Planning to visit Bithynia, God redirected him through a vision – a man begging, "Come over to Macedonia and help us," (Acts 16:6-10). This wasn't where Paul wanted to go, but it was where God wanted him. So Paul and his companions obeyed the Spirit.

As in most of Paul's travels, they gained converts, felt the blow of persecution, confronted spiritual evil, performed the supernatural, and in the end made it through by the hair of their chinny-chin-chins. God made them detour, but why? As the church in Macedonia grew and matured God's providing purpose came to life.

Sometime later, Jerusalem was struck by a severe famine. Paul wrote to the church in Corinth of the Macedonians' response to this calamity. "Out of the most severe trial, their overflowing joy and their extreme poverty welled up in rich generosity. For I testify that they gave as much as they were able, and even beyond their ability." (See 2 Corinthians 8:1-5). This ministry, established as a detour stop on Paul's second missionary journey, became a well spring through which God's blessings flowed.

When God sends you down roads less traveled, appearing to make little sense in your big picture and personal agenda, remember this: God sends no one on wild goose chases. Paul may have thought of this very detour when he wrote, "For all things work for the good, to those who love him and are called according to his purpose" (Romans 8:28). Your byway may be the pathway to another's answered prayers; the very connection God uses to bring future provision to you.

THE POSITION OF PROMINENCE

Growing up I was enthralled with sword fighting. Whether through the stories of King Arthur and the Knights of the Round Table, or the thieving adventures of Robin Hood and his merry men, or the armor-clad warriors of ancient Rome, the dueling battles of metallic blades captured was always a favorite.

Little has changed in 30 years. In truth, it requires little effort to remember the names of these mighty warriors. They were the embodiment of all that I wanted to be. But the stories included other players; people easier to ignore, those who faded into the scenery. They prepared food for banquets, cleaned up after horses, doing jobs or serving functions the gallant knights and noble kings had no time for.

I remember Lance-a-lot, Sir Gawain, Sir Galahad, and King Arthur, but I just can't recall one of those who served at their tables or brought their weaponry. My own memories or the lack of them, present a convicting fact – most want to be heroes, few choose to serve.

I didn't grow up wanting to be a mighty custodian, wielding a broom with grace, washing toilets with agility and skill. I never aspired to clean the barn; to maneuver through the manure of beasts and conquer the fields of grain. To be a waiter was never my aspiration, or doing a hard day's work in unnoticed, unappreciated obscurity.

Then Jesus steps in and declares, "Wait one minute! The ones you mentioned last shall be first, and the first shall be last" (Matthew 20:16). Those who serve, who may appear ordinary to the human eye, are the ones God sees as the true valiant warrior's and knights of legend.

Jesus told his disciples, "Whoever wants to be great among you must be your servant." (Matthew 20:26). But they didn't get it. Most of the time they dreamt about their places in the government of Jesus, arguing who was the greatest. Even when Jesus demonstrated what he met, it only confused them, angering some. As he washed their feet the lesson failed to travel to their minds.

Many modern disciples still find this hard to understand. But greatness is found still in service. Then again, a servant's heart is often not obtained in our normal schedules and routines. Only in the waiting and wandering moments do we learn our position.

Simon the Cyrene entered Jerusalem planning to worship in the temple, yet a detour led him to worship at the cross. He brought his two sons to see a sacrifice and so they did; the ultimate sacrifice. In this delay to their destination, God taught Simon to serve. He knelt to take the coarse beams of the cross from the Son of God. On his way to somewhere else he found the bloodied Messiah, and there he learned his true position.

Jesus told the story of a Samaritan delayed on the road from Jerusalem to Jericho. On the path before him lay a man robbed and left for dead. Twice this man's own people passed him, yet the Samaritan, "took pity on him ... bandaged his wounds ... put the man on his own donkey ... took him to an inn," then gave the inn keeper two silver coins and offered to pay any expenses the man accrued. (Luke 10:33-37). Before this incident the rescuer was just an unnamed Samaritan. What he learned in this delay would forever make his name synonymous with the word "good." And what did he learn? He learned his position, he learned to serve.

Serving often means obscurity; not needing recognition or applause; simply doing as the Master asks. In the Kingdom of God it is the "peasants," those who serve, who receive prominence.

Next time you are faced with a delay in your day or a detour in your schedule look around. There may be a divine appointment sitting at the table next to you or standing in the line behind you or watching your response to a bad situation. You may feel your time is being wasted, yet God has you exactly where he wants you. Your stoplight in life might be an opportunity to show someone the One who can bind up their spirit, heal their wounded heart, or satisfy the longing in their soul. Paul wrote to the church in Galatia, "Serve one another in love ... Carry each other's burdens and in this way you will fulfill the law of Christ." (Galatians 5:13 and 6:2).

THE PROTECTION OF THE LONGER ROUTE

At the end of your Bible, somewhere between the book of Revelation and the back cover hides an untapped resource of insight. At first glance they appear to be simple maps, but combined with careful study they offer much more. One such scrap of wisdom comes from combining Exodus chapter 13 and the corresponding map that illustrates the Exodus Trail. Go find your Bible and take a look at this map.

"Don't run past God ... you'll crash." – Ron Hutchcraft[61]

Now, note where Egypt is located and where the promise land of Canaan is, then draw a straight line. You will observe that the line you drew and the line that represents God's plan for Israel have only two things in common; the start and the finish. But nothing more.

The scriptures tell us, "When Pharaoh let the people go, God did not lead them on the road through the Philistine country, though that was shorter ... God led the people around by the desert road toward the Red Sea." (Exodus 13:17-18). Talk about a detour, using God's directions Moses led the people on a journey that was at least twice as long.

Why choose such a path? Because God wanted to protect them. The *IVP Bible Background Commentary* sheds a little more light on this, "The road through the Philistine country is a reference to the major route that ran through the Fertile Crescent ... the Egyptians referred to it as the Way of Horus and it was heavily defended since it was the route used by armies as well as trade caravans."[62]

Dr. Peter Enns in his commentary on the book of Exodus agrees, "The story takes an unexpected twist, however. God leads the Israelites on a path that they may not have expected – the longer route rather than the shorter ... (because) the shorter route will bring them into conflict with the Philistines."[63]

God led Israel the long way around to protect them from enemies from without and cowardice from within. God delivered them from Egypt, but he needed to defeat an enemy that was far greater, the Egypt within. He had to protect them from the short cut of discouragement and the fear of battle. He led them *His* way so that they would not go back to *theirs*.

God detours us for the same reasons. To protect us from something or someone he knows we cannot handle right now. He is kind and compassionate and aware of our weaknesses. Because of this the road he chooses for us at times, seems out of the way, but it's always for our good. We may not always understand why, but it may be the only way to get us from our Egypt to His Promised Land.

THE PERSPECTIVE OF THE PRODIGAL

An impatient young man left home – his inheritance in hand and delusions in his head. "Dad," he had demanded, "Give me my money now. I want to live life while I'm still young." But the party didn't last long. He squandered his wealth and watched his friends' rejection come as fast as his money left.

Now he sits in the pig slop, sizing up his self-made situation. "How many of my father's hired men have food to spare, and here I am starving to death! I will set out and go back to my father ..." (Luke 15:17-18). What once seemed too tame and old fashioned now became the desire of his heart. He wanted to go home. This pit stop in the pig pen brought the prodigal son a fresh perspective.

Detours and delays have a way of sharpening our vision. Full speed ahead distorts our outlook, but a pause brings remarkable clarity. We see things differently. We notice what we once ignored.

How we see life is often more powerful than the facts. When our perspective is skewed it can disrupt how we feel and what we believe. Assuming something about someone or a situation produces a variety of results, most often bad. Our perspective can lead us astray – the way we see things taking power over reality.

Like the prodigal we may need a "time-out" to see things clearly. Or a pause in the action to gain better understanding. As we wait, God can lift us up on wings like eagles in order to show us life from a higher vantage point ... a new perspective.

TAKE THE DETOUR – IT MAY LEAD TO A DREAM COME TRUE!

Joseph dreamt he would be great – he just never dreamed the journey would take so long ... and be so hard. The visions came to him as a young man of seventeen. But God had much to do between the revelation and the fulfillment. The Lord had established Joseph's future, but Joseph had to be made ready.

155

Follow the path of Joseph's detour. It began with betrayal and slavery. But then gradually climbed as he experienced success. Soon, however, his journey dipped down into the valley of false accusations and imprisonment. Even there he found promotion and an introduction that provided hope of freedom — only to be forgotten.

For two years he traveled this dark tunnel until finally, the brightness of day arrived as his path took him to the top of the Egyptian government. Over seven years passed and his dream came true – his brothers bow before him, now Zaphenath-paneah, "God speaks and guides," the governor of Egypt.

Joseph allowed himself to be molded on the Potter's wheel of divine delay and detour. And "the Lord was with him," every step of the way (Genesis 39:3 and 23) … Just like He is with you and me.

Every delay and detour has a purpose. The reasons may vary, but take heart they exist. As we've learned in our journey thus far, we are better off if we let God be God and take our place in the shelter of his Divine wisdom. Our travels will go much smoother if we leave the driving to Him. Next time you face a Divine Delay or Detour put these three principles into practice …

1. *View them as GIFTS* – Obstacles or opportunities, it all depends on how you see them!
2. *Look for the LESSON within each one* – Every stop has something to teach us, if we are willing to look for it!
3. *Be willing to let them CHANGE you* – Theses gifts and lessons do us no good unless we allow them to transform us!

In reality there are no detours with God, just a path that he lays out before us and the unfortunate alternatives. We can trust the one who guides us even when we don't understand the delay, for he promises, "I know the plans I have for you declares the Lord; plans to prosper you not to harm you; plans to give you a future and a hope." (Jeremiah 29:11).

DISCUSSING DELAYS AND DETOURS:

1. How does it help to know that God has a purpose in the delays and detours of your life?

2. When you face these stops how can you prevent yourself from becoming distracted by the circumstances? How can you be more aware of what God may be trying to teach you?

3. How can you begin to see delays and detours for their opportunities instead of as obstacles?

4. Next time you face a waiting period don't waste it – ask God what he is trying to reveal to you? What might happen if you choose not to learn from a detour?

5. Think back to a time you had to wait? What lesson(s) did you learn from that delay? Who might God have in your life who could be encouraged by this?

Stop #12

ONE FOR THE ROAD – A FEW LESSONS COOKED UP "TO GO"

Few experiences compare to the satisfaction of a good meal – the rare moment when our expectations and our experiences match perfectly. We push back from the table, feeling content. With an extended stretch and a smile spreading across our faces we say those seldom spoken yet treasured words, "That hit the spot." Where the spot is, I'm not quite sure, but when it gets hit … you know it.

Not wanting such an experience to end, we ask the waitress one final request. She kindly obliges setting the box, bag, or tin foil on our table. We pay our bill and head out the door. Our leftovers in hand, carefully made ready to go.

Like that meal I hope this book has been one of those occasions that hit the spot. Before we go our separate ways there are a few final traveling instructions I would like to "wrap up" for you to take on your journey. So here's one more for the road, a few thoughts cooked up to go.

"Know the true value of time; snatch, seize, enjoy
every moment of it. No idleness, no laziness, no

procrastination; never put off tomorrow what you can do today." Lord Chesterfield[64]

DON'T FIGHT THE JOURNEY

When I was eleven my Dad "requested" my help with a project that held as much appeal as the smell it secreted. The front lawn had begun to grow greener than ever before, unfortunately the lush foliage was accompanied by a pungent stench. It was apparent something was wrong. Dad explained to my brother and me that the septic tank must be damaged. Then he handed us a few shovels and a pick and said, "Dig in!" (Dad certainly did his fair share of work too, I might add).

"There are two kinds of people: Those who say to God, 'Thy will be done,' and those to whom God says, 'All right, then, have it your way'" – C.S. Lewis[65]

It was an unusually hot summer day when we began our project; making the task even less pleasant. Like gold miners we scratched at the ground, but glimmers of gold dust were not what we found. The deeper we dug, the more nauseating the fumes rising from the wet soil. Reaching the base of the septic tank revealed the problem.

The drain field pipes were not plastic but concrete. Over time the putrefying sludge left them in ruins, disintegrated to crumbling fragments. The sewage, now undirected and free to flow, was seeping its way closer to the house.

Correcting this problem was a journey I wanted nothing to do with, nonetheless it was necessary. Fighting it would have only made our lives more unpleasant; the smell driving us from our home.

To refuse to comply held other consequences; obstinacy and disobedience always do. And in the end I would've been forced to travel the road I loathed anyway. Fighting the journey only makes the process harder and longer; it makes life stink. Just ask Jonah.

You are probably familiar with the story of the wrong way prophet swallowed by an aggressive God-sent fish. If not, his story can be found in appropriately, the Old Testament book Jonah.

In short, God had a mission for Jonah. He wanted this prophet to travel to the city of Nineveh to warn the people to repent or face God's wrath. However, Jonah chose to set off in the exact opposite direction.

Jonah had his reasons for running, just like you and I do. Perhaps anger, selfishness, or because he thought he knew better than God. After all, why should he, a prophet of the Most High God, help evil foreigners? Why be concerned for their welfare? So Jonah ran, or rather floated away from God's will. But there is no ship, plane, train, or automobile fast enough to escape God. We cannot avoid the journey.

> *"We cannot get away from God, though we can ignore him" – James Elliot Cabot*[66]

In all of his fighting, Jonah only made the journey more difficult. God's purpose for Jonah's life and the Ninevites would come to pass regardless of Jonah's efforts to stop it. After a raging storm nearly sank his ship, Jonah was tossed overboard, spent three nights in the belly of a great fish, and was then hurled up on the beach outside the city. God's will was accomplished — the entire city repented — and all Jonah had to show for his troubles was a personal account of what happens inside a fishes stomach, a unique smell, and a good lesson; don't fight the journey.

Jonah discovered that fighting the journey only made for futility and fishiness. When we choose to fight the journey we'll find the same result. Like Jonah, and my septic situation, fighting only makes life stink and forces the discipline of the Father. So we might as well enjoy the journey, we certainly can't avoid it.

KEEP YOUR BALANCE

Even as I wrote this book a caution light continued to flash in my mind. Even as I recover from living "Destination Driven," it is hard for me to imagine anyone falling into this category. But just in case you're out there. Please read this warning.

There are some who may use the Journey Focused philosophy as an excuse to float through life without a care in the world or plan for the future. You just might see "enjoying the journey" as justification to put your boat in the water and just sit there. Perhaps like a famous animated Lion you've adopted the lifestyle of "Hakuna Matata,"[67] a life of no worries and no responsibilities.

While it is true, God teaches us much on the way, this is not a passive activity. From the gospels, Jesus taught "do not worry," but that's not all. God has a plan and a dream for your life. Some of that includes relaxation and observation, but it doesn't end there. He gave us a Great Commission and Great Commandments that are only accomplished as we do our part.

Don't confuse faith with laziness or journeying with complacency — procrastination and apathy are unacceptable ways to travel. To do nothing is to place ourselves in the same unenviable position as the man who was given one talent by his master and buried it (Matthew 25:25). The balanced traveler journeys neither in self-reliance nor laziness, rather through God-directed activity and diligent faith he or she pursues God's purpose.

Someone once said, "If you aim at nothing, you're sure to hit it." The Apostle Paul agreed, "Therefore I do not run like a man running aimlessly; I do not fight like a man beating the air." (I Corinthians 9:26). We have a target to shoot at, a focus to fix on, and a prize to gain. So jump in the boat and enjoy the journey, but take a paddle. We do, after all, have a destination.

"Laziness is sometimes mistaken for patience."
– French Saying[68]

KEEP A STEADY PACE

A friend of mine once trained young people to compete in marathons. Every year at the first practice he gave no instruction. He just simply told them they were running 5 miles.

The result was always the same. The young men headed out first at the fastest pace. Within a mile Dan would catch up with them all, typically on the side of the road gasping for air and nauseated. The exhausted students listened much better to the teacher at this point as he shared an important life lesson with the team — keep a steady pace.

> *"The race is not to the swift ... but time and chance happen to them all." Ecclesiastes 9:11*

Life is no different. To be a successful traveler depends more on your pace than your initial speed. As you approach every leg of your journey make sure to take a break at times, push hard at times, but always understand what time it is, so that you don't burn out or fade away. There is a time to walk and a time to run, have the wisdom to know which you should be doing in each season you face.

The Apostle Paul said, "Run in such a way as to get the prize" (see 1 Corinthians 9:24-26). That means we go into strict training, don't get entangled by the things that can weigh us down, focus on the Leader, and take life one step at a time (see Hebrews 12:1-2). In a race, all runners run to get a prize, not everyone wins but all can finish; if they keep a steady pace.

CHASE A DREAM

The movie, *Rudy* traces the life of a young man and his obsession with Notre Dame Football. Though possessed great heart, Rudy was cursed with a smallish body and an undisciplined mind. He strove to make his way after high school working at a steel mill. But the dream wouldn't die. On his 21st birthday his best friend Pete shared a statement with him that stoked the embers of his passion. He said, "Having dreams is what makes life tolerable."

> *"There are worse things in life to be called than a courageous dreamer ... The challenge is to have the vision to dream ... and the courage, persistence, and patience to turn that dream into reality." — Former President Ronald Reagan*[69]

In the midst of the journey the joy of life can sometimes be lost. Crowded offices, jammed back streets, long lines, over committed schedules, late nights, and early mornings, can rob us of fulfillment and happiness — washing away some of the promise once envisioned. But there is something that can restart our joy and recharge our zest for life. DREAMS.

I've felt their power in my own barrenness; when my back tired under the burden and my soul longed for more than the routine. Ministry is wonderful but it has its challenges. There are times I can feel the drain, bogged down by carrying the cares of others. Then it happens; out of nowhere, quite unexpected, God hits me with a dream.

My pulse races, my heart pounds faster, and the exasperation I felt moments earlier is replaced with revived energy and excitement. There is nothing as life changing as God directed, God birthed, God breathed dreams.

What dream has God put in your heart? What vision has he placed before your eyes? What has he called you to do that is so far beyond you that it both terrifies and thrills you – all at the same time? Oh, I know you have your reasons for not trying and I know others have told you, *"You don't have what it takes."* So what? If you fail, you'll gain a whole new truck load of experiences and lessons from the journey, and in truth you're no worse off.

Let the "Nay-sayers" have their say, you follow God's dream. Remember Joseph. People didn't appreciate his visions either, even those closest to him. "Here comes that dreamer," his older brothers spat with disdain in their voices and jealousy in their hearts. But that didn't stop the dream (Genesis 37:19).

Rudy had his detractors too. His own father tried to dissuade him, "Chasing a stupid dream causes nothing but you and everyone around you heartache." He then went on to list all the reasons others might succeed but why Rudy could not. When a well meaning priest tried to do the same Rudy explained, "My whole life people have told me what I could and couldn't do. I always believed them ... But I want to stop believing."[70]

*"He who says something is impossible should get out of
the way of he who is doing it" Chinese Proverb[71]*

If God gives you a dream it is more than possible, it's in the bag,
as long as you choose to follow. Listen to the Word of God, let him
speak life and reject the lies ...

"I can do everything through him who gives me strength."
— Philippians 4:13

*"No eye has seen, no ear has heard, no mind has conceived
what God has prepared for those who love him" — I
Corinthians 2:9*

*"I tell you the truth, anyone who has faith in me will do what
I have been doing. He will do even greater things than these,
because I am going to the Father." — John 14:12*

Greater than Jesus? Well, that should keep us from getting too
bored, don't you think? What an amazing dream he left us, in those
words alone! Reach the lost, heal the sick, preach the good news,
stand for truth, and touch your world. Whether you are a housewife
or a CEO, God has a dream for you. It may not make sense to *you*,
but it fits into *His* plan. Dreams may cost, but not following costs
more. The only question is will you go?

In 1976 Danil E. "Rudy" Ruettiger graduated from Notre Dame
University with a Bachelors degree. He played in a real football
game for Notre Dame and was carried off the field in celebration
on the shoulders of his teammates. Today, Rudy is a widely sought
after motivational speaker who still believes, "Dreaming is a lifetime occupation."[71]

Rudy realized his dream because he chased it with all his heart.
Will you? Joseph's dreams came true because he trusted God,
ignored the criticism and attacks of others, and walked in faithful
obedience through the process. Will you? Champions come and go
but the underdog; the undersized that won't give up but keep fighting

for an impossible dream never fade away. God loves to use dreamers who have nothing but faith in him and a little bit of moxie.

YOU'RE NEVER ALONE

Greek mythology tells the story of a massive immortal known as Atlas. Enlisting the help of his fellow Titans, Atlas led a revolt against the gods of Olympus. Though the war was costly for both sides, Atlas and his companions fell in defeat. As punishment he was forced to hold up the world upon his shoulders, all alone.[72] You may have seen his likeness in art, as I did as a boy. My hope is that you're not living out his sentence in your journey.

No matter what you face in life or where your journey takes you, you are never alone. The writer of Hebrews, referring to the Old Testament promise of God from Deuteronomy, wrote, "Never will I leave you, never will I forsake you." (Hebrews 13:5). Jesus encouraged his disciples saying, "Surely I am with you always, to the very end of the age." (Matthew 28:20). The prophet Isaiah penned these words hundreds of years before the birth of Christ, "Can a mother forget the baby at her breast and have no compassion on the child she has born? Though she may forget, I will not forget you." (Isaiah 49:15)

> *"What matter supremely, therefore, is not the fact that I know God, but that he knows me. I am graven on the palms of His hands. I am never out of His mind ... and there is no moment when his eye is off me, or his attention distracted from me, and no moment, therefore, when his care falters ... God is constantly taking knowledge of me in love and watching over me ... No discovery now can disillusion Him about me (nor) quench his determination to bless me." – J.I. Packer, <u>Knowing God</u>*

There will be times that we wander through the dryness of the dessert, through setbacks, and temptation; times when our faith will be tested walking on the stormy seas of life – when we feel alone. But the fact remains, Jesus is with us. Nothing can separate us from the love of God in Christ Jesus (Romans 8:39). No one walks alone.

As the path before you weaves and turns and winds its way through life's many adventures, hold tightly to the hand of Jesus – look to him, "so that you will not grow weary and lose heart." (Hebrews 12:3).

Unlike Atlas we're not required to carry our burden alone. The weight of our journey rests on another. It is cradled securely on the shoulders of Christ.

THOSE LOST ON THE WAY

Many travel the paths we trod. Many look confused, darting here and there like caged birds seeking the door to freedom. Others appear lost, searching for the way home. Some give off an air of pride as they flounder about acting as if they know the way. Others reveal fear and uncertainty weaving from one road to the next. Yet, if they have not found the "Road Maker" all are lost.

Notice them, look closely. In them you will see the resemblance of the Creator, for they too were made in his image. The cause for their wandering? They are blind. "The God of this age has blinded the minds of unbelievers, so that they cannot see the light of the gospel of the glory of Christ, who is the image of God." (2 Corinthians 4:4). They need someone to point them toward home; you and me.

This is our greatest calling; to be the "light of the world," the "salt of the earth," to carry out our mission to "go" and "seek and save the lost." Jesus said, "I am the way, the truth, and the life, no man comes home to the father accept through me." (John 14:6, 10:9; Matthew 5:13-16)

All followers of Christ are headed home, but what a celebration it could be if we determined to lead others there as Jesus commissioned. In the end that is exactly what the journey is all about; leading as many home to our Heavenly Father as possible ... to our Final Destination.

"Go out at once into the streets and the lanes of the city and bring in here the poor and the crippled and the lame

*... Go out into the highways and along the hedges and
compel them to come in, so that my house may be filled."
– Jesus[73]*

Perhaps you have read this book and still have yet to choose
Jesus Christ to be your Guide and your Savior. I invite you right
now to join me and take the journey. You need not wait for a pastor
or a church service. The God of the journey is with you now. Speak
to him and he will listen; call on him and he will answer; invite him
into your journey and he will come and be with you (Revelation
3:20, Acts 2:21, John 3:16). I've included a prayer, but all you need
are the words from your heart.

*Dear Jesus, Thank you for making me and seeking
to save my life. I have journeyed many years trying to
do things my way but today I choose you. I have made
mistakes and chosen to do wrong, I ask for your forgiveness. I now realize that because of the sins I have
committed you took your own journey to the cross long
ago. I thank you for dying for my sins and for rising
from the dead to make my pardon possible and my hope
complete. I confess Jesus Christ is Lord and believe you
are alive today I ask you to guide and direct my life and to
give me courage to walk with you. Jesus, thank you for all
you've done. I choose today to serve you. Give me a new
heart and a fresh start, In Jesus Name Amen!*

If you prayed that prayer from your heart to God's I want to assure
you he heard every word. Right now in heaven there is "rejoicing
in the presence of angels" (Luke 15:10). God himself is celebrating
and it's all because of you. Welcome to the family!

Find a Bible believing, Bible teaching church where you can ask
questions and learn more about this new life you've entered into.

To all of you who have chosen to take this journey with me,
Thank you. My prayer is that God will bring the lessons of these
pages back to your mind (as he has with me) as you venture into
new frontiers. God bless you in all your "on the ways." Enjoy the

journey. And if I never meet you here on this earth, I'll see you when we get Home.

> *"We were made for something greater, but it takes a journey to discover what that is." C.S. Lewis*[74]

A FEW QUESTIONS LEFTOVER:

1. What are some ways you will endeavor to live a balanced life, both doing what God wants you to do and being who God wants you to be?

2. What are some things you can do to ensure that you pace yourself over the long haul?

3. What dream has God placed in your life? Are you pursuing it or have you stopped? Have other spoken "death" into your dream? Ask God to renew his dream for you or to give you a fresh dream?

4. Is there something in your journey that you are running from? Is there a person you need to forgive, something you need to give, a direction you need to follow, or a kind word of encouragement you need to say? Ask the Lord to reveal to you if he has something right now for you to learn that you are missing.

5. Who do you know that is lost on the way? Commit to pray for that person asking God to draw them to himself and give you the continued opportunity to show God's love.

6. Read James 3:13-18 and Philippians 2:3-4. How might these passages direct your dream to make sure it is a godly dream and not worldly ambition? Make a list below that may help you keep your dream on the straight and narrow.

Endnotes

1. Associated Press Article by Calvin Woodward, published in the Helena Independent Record, May 30, 2006
2. The Pentecostal Evangel Magazine, Published May 14, 2006
3. Ibid
4. Article, *"Stressed out and Sick About it,"* written by Karen Pallarito on www.health.nmhs.net
5. Ibid
6. Ibid
7. Used by permission from *With This Ring: Promises to Keep,* by Joanna Weaver (Colorado Springs, Colorado, Waterbrook Press, 2000)
8. Quote found from, www.thinkexist.com
9. Quote found from, www.thinkexist.com
10. *Desiring God: Meditations of a Christian Hedonist,* By John Piper (Sisters Oregon, Multnomah, 1996) p. 15
11. *Finishing Strong,* by Steve Farrar (Sisters Oregon, Multnomah, 2000)
12. www.startrek.com
13. *The Tale of the Tardy Oxcart,* by Charles R, Swindoll (Nashville, Tennessee Word Puplishing,1998) p. 278
14. *Quotationary*, Leonard Roy Frank, Editor (New York, NY, Random House Webster's, 1999) p. 374
15. Ibid
16. *14,000 Quips & Quotes*, compiled by E.C. McKenzie (Grand Rapid, Michigan, Baker Book House, 1980)

17. Adapted from *Baron's How to Prepare For the CLEP*, by Doster, Rozakis, Griffith, and Ward (Hauppauge, NY, Barren's Educational Series 2003)
18. From the movie, *National Treasure*, Walt Disney Pictures Inc., 2004
19. *12,000 Religious Quotations*, edited and compiled by Frank S. Mead (Grand Rapids, Michigan, Baker House Books, 1989) p. 189
20. The Hymn, *Tis So Sweet To Trust in Jesus*, by Louisa M. R. Stead
21. *The Complete C.S. Lewis Signature Classics*, (New York, NY, HarperSanFrancisco 2002) p. 35
22. *14,000 Quips & Quotes*, compiled by E.C. McKenzie (Grand Rapid, Michigan, Baker Book House, 1980) p. 177
23. Ibid
24. Hebrews 13:15
25. Matthew 28:20
26. News Article by New York Times columnist Nicholas Kristoff, 2005
27. *12,000 Religious Quotations*, edited and compiled by Frank S. Mead (Grand Rapids, Michigan, Baker House Books, 1989) p. 163
28. News Article by New York Times columnist Nicholas Kristoff, 2005
29. *12,000 Religious Quotations*, edited and compiled by Frank S. Mead (Grand Rapids, Michigan, Baker House Books, 1989) p. 179
30. *14,000 Quips & Quotes*, compiled by E.C. McKenzie (Grand Rapid, Michigan, Baker Book House, 1980)
31. *Illustrations Unlimited*, James S. Hewett, Editor (Wheaton, Illinois Tyndale House Publishers, 1988) p. 467
32. *12,000 Religious Quotations*, edited and compiled by Frank S. Mead (Grand Rapids, Michigan, Baker House Books, 1989) p. 429
33. Author's Files

34. *The Right to Lead: A Study in Character and Courage*, by John C. Maxwell (Nashville, Tennessee J Countryman, Thomas Nelson, 2001) p. 53

35. *The Right to Lead: A Study in Character and Courage*, by John C. Maxwell (Nashville, Tennessee, J. Countryman, Thomas Nelson, 2001) p. 89

36. *Strong's Complete Dictionary of Bible Words*, James Strong LL.D., S.T.D. (Nashville, Tennessee, Thomas Nelson, 1996)

37. James 1:14-15

38. Romans 7:21-24

39. Author's files

40. Found from, www.thinkexist.com

41. *12,000 Religious Quotations*, edited and compiled by Frank S. Mead (Grand Rapids, Michigan, Baker House Books, 1989) p. 439

42. As quoted from a wall hanging by Successories Inc

43. *Quotationary*, Leonard Roy Frank, Editor (New York, NY, Random House Webster's, 1999) p. 457

44. Article, *"A Relevant Gospel in a Scientific Age,"* by Paul A. Bartz, 1985 found at www.creationmoments.net

45. *Quotationary*, Leonard Roy Frank, Editor (New York, NY, Random House Webster's, 1999) p. 511

46. Story heard in a Sermon at Spring Break-A-Way, 2001, Bozeman Montana

47. *Illustrations Unlimited*, James S. Hewett, Editor (Wheaton, Illinois Tyndale House Publishers, 1988) p. 187

48. *The Tale of the Tardy Oxcart,* by Charles R, Swindoll (Nashville, Tennessee Word Puplishing,1998) p. 375

49. As heard from a sermon by Reverend Rick Ross, Glacier Bible Camp, Hungry Horse Montana, May 2005

50. *Quotationary*, Leonard Roy Frank, Editor (New York, NY, Random House Webster's, 1999) p. 235

51. *Nelson's Complete Book of Stories, Illustrations, & Quotes*, Robert J. Morgan (Nashville, Tennessee Thomas Nelson Publishers, 2000) p. 635

52. *Carry A Big Stick: The Uncommon Heroism of Theodore Roosevelt*, by George Grant (Nashville, Tennessee, Cumberland House Publishing, 1996) p. 121

53. The Hymn, *What a Friend We Have in Jesus*, by Joseph Medlicott Scriven

54. *Quotationary*, Leonard Roy Frank, Editor (New York, NY, Random House Webster's, 1999)

55. *Carry A Big Stick: The Uncommon Heroism of Theodore Roosevelt*, by George Grant (Nashville, Tennessee, Cumberland House Publishing, 1996) p. 79

56. *Why Enter Heaven Unannounced*, by Angela Lougee (Xulon Press, 2004)

57. A quote by Mark Lowry as heard in concert

58. *Why Enter Heaven Unannounced*, by Angela Lougee (Xulon Press, 2004)

59. *Enjoying Where You Are On The Way To Where You Are Going*, by Joyce Meyer (Fenton, Missouri, Warner Books, 1996)

60. *Strong's Complete Dictionary of Bible Words*, James Strong LL.D., S.T.D. (Nashville, Tennessee, Thomas Nelson, 1996)

61. Author's files

62. *The IVP Background Commentary; Old Testament*, by Walton, Matthews, and Chavalas (Downers Grove, Illinois, InterVarsity Press, 2000) p. 89

63. The NIV Application Commentary, By Dr. Peter Enns (Grand Rapids, Michigan, Zondervan Publishing House, 2000) p. 269

64. *Quotationary*, Leonard Roy Frank, Editor (New York, NY, Random House Webster's, 1999) p. 660

65. *12,000 Religious Quotations*, edited and compiled by Frank S. Mead (Grand Rapids, Michigan, Baker House Books, 1989)

66. *12,000 Religious Quotations*, edited and compiled by Frank S. Mead (Grand Rapids, Michigan, Baker House Books, 1989)

67. From the movie *The Lion King* by Walt Disney Pictures Inc., 1994

68. *Quotationary*, Leonard Roy Frank, Editor (New York, NY, Random House Webster's, 1999) p. 440

69. Quotable Reagan, by Steve Eubanks (Nashville Tennessee, TowleHouse Publishing, 2001) p. 57 and 70

70. All quotes and reference taken from the movie *Rudy*, TriStar Pictures Inc., 1993
71. www.chasingthefrog.com
72. Microsoft Encarta 98 Encyclopedia, Microsoft Co. Seattle Washington
73. Luke 14:21-23
74. Author's Files

Printed in the United States
142279LV00004B/2/P

9 781607 914907